To Evalie Brock

Many Thanks for your interest
Journey" & for he-Connecting Marilyn
& myself with old friends and our
LeClaire tours!

Wild Journey

On the trail with a Wyoming game warden in Yellowstone Country

May There always be wildlife
& wild places To calm The
human Spirit!

Best Wishes,

Dave Bragonier

WordsWorth
Cody, Wyoming

Wild Journey

On the trail with a Wyoming game warden in Yellowstone Country

Dave Bragonier

Published by WordsWorth
1285 Sheridan Avenue, Suite 275
Cody, Wyoming   82414

Library of Congress Card Number : 99-071407

ISBN 0-9652942-3-4

Printed in the United States of America on acid-free paper.

To my lovely wife, Germaine, always the gracious hostess,
game warden station information officer and mother;
and to Cheryl, Brian and Scott,
who spent many evenings, weekends and holidays
without their Dad.

Table of Contents

Preface

I am very fortunate to have spent most of my game warden years in the Yellowstone country. During those years I had many enjoyable experiences, although a few encounters were not so pleasant.

Some folks have suggested that I publish my memoirs so others might also ride along on those adventures. This inducement, alone, would never have prodded me into such an undertaking.

There are, however, several current wildlife related issues of national importance that deeply concern me. The book idea became a reality when I decided to use it as a vehicle to interject my two-cents-worth into these significant ongoing debates.

Since my first day on the job, I've kept personal journals to record pertinent information and interesting events so that I could accurately file my required monthly reports with the Wyoming Game and Fish Department. Because I still possess all those journals, together with my copies of arrest records, game management and other data gathered during that time, I had more than my memory to refer to while working on the project.

As the cyberspace age matured, the game and fish department attempted to make computer geeks out of all game wardens despite the hollering and grumbling from the older officers. We predicted a number of awful things would happen because of this new-fangled science, including the demise of the civilized world – a forecast still not too far-fetched. At least one of our predictions has came to pass: the mandatory time now spent fiddling on computers has taken game wardens out of the field where they are desperately needed. This sort of change helped me to decide that it was time to hang it up. Then, simultaneous with my decision to retire, danged if I didn't "inherit" a computer from my daughter, Cheryl, when she upgraded her system. She said it would make the task of writing a book much easier. It still hurts whenever I must admit that it did!

One issue of considerable importance to me is the current grizzly bear dilemma. Bitter debates continue on whether to delist the bear from its "threatened" status under the federal Endangered Species Act. Some folks argue for full protection of the species from this day forward. Still others desire eradication of the grizzly.

We must not allow this magnificent animal to vanish from the West. At least for me, the grizzly bear represents true Rocky Mountain wilderness. Because I truly believe it to be imperative that we take a realistic and commonsense approach to the animal's management, considerable space between these covers has been devoted to this discussion.

Within is a history of grizzly-human conflicts, and their likely causes, in the Yellowstone Ecosystem and elsewhere. Several grizzly mauling case investigations are related. Here, I make a few suggestions pertaining to proper backcountry etiquette and techniques that might help users of grizzly bear habitat to return safely to the front county. Readers are told about the identifying characteristics of both black and grizzly bears, along with some of the analogies and variations of those species. All users of grizzly habitat must practice good wilderness ethics if bear and man are to coexist.

Another, much uglier, debate is rapidly gaining speed on the national front. It is the battle between the hunting and anti-hunting communities.

Sport hunting is coming under increasing attack because too many hunters lack ethics and continue to exhibit disregard for conservation laws. This moral decay within the sportsmen's community also includes more than a few anglers. Hunting has long been chastised by the anti-hunting crowd. But now, many non-hunters are also beginning to question the validity of sport hunting and certain fishing techniques because of what's occurring. And the hard truth is that there are few true sportsmen out there! It's wake up time for them. Hunters must demonstrate more respect for the law and the land if they expect positive consideration from the non-hunting public. Just how far into the next millennium sport hunting can be enjoyed is mostly up to the hunting fraternity.

This very important concern is given considerable space because I believe that ethical hunting is a more humane method of wildlife population control than is either disease or famine.

This book would not be complete without a discussion of the black marketeers who poach and deal in wildlife for illegal monetary gain. Alongside these low-lifes are the thieves who poach for lust alone. Here, please allow for a certain amount of author bias.

However, *Wild Journey* tells more than game warden war stories. Wyoming game wardens are both wildlife cops and game managers. The narrative tells of the dangers, frustrations and rewards that go with the territory of a mountain wildlife officer. It relates behind-the-scene and straightforward accounts of a warden's journeys. Of course all accounts are true, and many of the incidents take place in the shadow of the Teton Mountains and at other locations within the Yellowstone region.

My interest in western history surfaces in *Tom Vernon Remembers Butch Cassidy* and at other locations along the trail.

One duty of a Wyoming warden is the handling of game damage complaints and claims under Wyoming's liberal game damage laws and regulations. The game damage story and others such as the *"You Owe Us!"* account will give readers a better look at a game warden's real world.

During the span of my career, wildlife has lost much of its habitat throughout the world. At the same time, wildlife management and game law enforcement practices and methodologies have undergone significant change. These transformations include large-scale recruitment by game departments of wildlife specialists of every job description imaginable, spectacular advances in law enforcement training and techniques such as police science college degree programs, and the DNA testing science.

There have been many federal and state laws enacted for the benefit of wildlife. Those years were also witness to dramatic growth in the environmental movement which now has a loud and powerful political voice. These environmental watch dogs deserve credit for causing needed change in many of the old and wasteful methods of natural resource management. And, of course, the anti-hunters have formed into many rabid and drooling packs in their relentless attempt to hamstring hunters.

The scientific community's many contributions benefiting wildlife are always well documented and publicized. However, misinterpretations and damaging research procedures which occurred during the evolution of wildlife management are understandably not as well publicized. To err is only human, and no one is immune from it. But there are also those who are so wrapped up in themselves that they sometimes fail to reach accurate and rational conclusions because of it. And such individuals are found within every profession.

It may be of equal importance, albeit embarrassing, to record for posterity the potentially damaging mistakes and improprieties, in hopes of preventing them from reoccurring.

With this in mind, I relate the *"What Have We Done To The Grizzly Bear!"* story. This is the story that many "hands-on" bear researchers had hoped would never be told! Readers will also find documented within, the not-so-ancient scientific belief that sagebrush is good for little. Both accounts are valuable lessons not to be forgotten!

Incorporated into the work is the intriguing account of the mysterious murders of two Wyoming game wardens who were slain in the Sierra Madre Mountains of southern Wyoming in 1945. I believe this to be the first in-depth account of the murders ever told.

If wildlife and its habitat has benefited even in some small way, the wild journey will have been worthwhile!

Enjoy!

DJB

Acknowledgments

A special thanks to Marik Berghs. But for her enthusiasm and encouragement this may have never happened!

Many thanks to my old friend and comrade Tim Fagan for the use of his great photo, shown on the cover, depicting game warden Jerry Longobardi and his buddies near where Beaver Dam Creek enters Yellowstone Lake. I also wish to extend my sincere appreciation to my dear friend and noted Western artist Dee Smith for the use of his excellent work on the title page.

Thanks to the following individuals who shared their time, knowledge and resources with me while I undertook this project. I apologize to those who may have been overlooked.

Randy Blackburn, Cody, Wyoming
Gene Carrico, Rawlins, Wyoming
Oscar Hall, Rawlins, Wyoming
Calvin King, Thermopolis, Wyoming
Dr. Scott Moore, Cody, Wyoming
William Nichols, LeClaire, Iowa
Jim Oudin, Cody, Wyoming
Ray Ring, Rawlins, Wyoming
Milo Vukelich, Helena, Montana
Ted Williams, Grafton, Massachusetts
James Yorgason, Cody, Wyoming
National Park Service:
     Kate Kendall
U.S. Fish & Wildlife Service:
     Tim Eicher
U.S. Forest Service:
     Andy Norman, Dave Myers and Judy Robinson
Wyoming Game & Fish Department:

Lin Bashford	Duane Hyde
Gary Brown	Jay Lawson
Mark Bruscino	Ron McKnight
Terry Cleveland	Robert Pistono
Duke Early	Larry Roop
Tim Fagan	Gary Shorma
Fred Herbel	Steve Yekel

Jackson Hole Trails

Bill Daniels, Mountain Man

At some point in most boys' young lives, they dream of becoming cowboys or forest rangers so they can ride the range and catch their breakfast from a mountain stream. The majority of these lads soon outgrow this desire. I never did.

During my senior year in high school, Dad had grown hoarse, to no avail, expounding to me the many virtues of really becoming somebody; a doctor, a lawyer or such. He at least persuaded me to enroll at Iowa State for the coming fall term. I know, though, that he was disappointed when I elected to attend their forestry school.

That summer, I landed a seasonal job as a fire guard on the Teton National Forest in western Wyoming. I was assigned to the Goosewing ranger district, on the Gros Ventre River, and soon found that a fire guard's main duty in ranger Bob Safran's district was policing Forest Service campgrounds and roadways, otherwise known as trash collecting. I did, however, spend a month manning Deer Creek Fire Lookout during August of that first year.

Bob and I got along super, though, and I followed him over to the Blackrock Ranger District the following year. That's where I first met T.W. "Bill" Daniels.

Safran told me that I would be working with the grizzled old mountain man in the Teton Primitive Area that summer. I would be assisting Bill with backcountry trail maintenance and other duties such as firefighting efforts later on during the dry season on the "Asbestos Forest" as the Teton was then known. We would headquarter out of the remote Hawks Rest patrol station at Bridger Lake near the border of Yellowstone National Park. I was elated! Imagine spending the summer on horseback, and 30 miles from the nearest road.

Bill had worked, seasonally, many years for the Forest Service as a backcountry ranger doing trail maintenance, packing, fire-fighting, and "a-trainin'" a good many rangers in the ways of the mountains. During the winter he was a special deputy warden for the Wyoming Game and Fish Department, and also fed elk and moose at Blackrock.

T.W. "Bill" Daniels on Red Cloud at Enos Lake Forest Service patrol cabin. Photo: Dave Bragonier

Daniels was of medium stature, with a husky build and was about 60 years of age at the time. He had a deep, gruff voice which most folks heeded, especially if you were still wet behind the ears. One of the first things I noticed about him was the absence of the three fingers between the thumb and little finger of his left hand. And that little finger was not so little!

Ranger Safran confided to me that most kids didn't get along too well with Bill because he wouldn't stand for any monkey business, and because he also expected them to hold up their end when it came to working, both on the trail and around camp. Daniels had seen more than his share of college kids through the years, and I'm sure that he was saying to himself, "I'm gettin' stuck with another one of them damned lazy kids!"

I realized that I could learn a great deal from this hardy veteran, and resolved to do my part to get along with him. Bill told me later that it seemed to him, "Most kids now-a-days are smart-mouthed know-it-alls who think they don't have to work 'cause they're goin' ta college!"

He continued, "I may have only gone through the fifth grade, but I was taught early on that ya gotta carry yer own weight in this o' life, and they don't seem ta teach that anywhere, anymore."

Bill and I got along well, and worked together, off and on, for the next three seasons. And I learned a great deal from him, mostly from watching, as he didn't explain much; that is, unless you screwed up. I found that, like many other able mountain men, he seemed a little possessive of his wealth of backcountry knowledge and horse savvy. These men knew that what they may have lacked in formal training, they possessed in valuable skills that were still needed in a few remote places.

During many pleasant evenings around the campfire, I learned much about this interesting old-timer. He had been born and raised on a homestead near Coburg, Oregon, around the turn of the century. In addition to farming, his father drove a stagecoach route in the Willamette Valley. As a youth, Daniels had worked on the farm, and sometimes hunted cougars with hounds in the nearby hills.

About the time of World War I, Bill and his brothers Larry, Shorty, and Slim took homesteads on Horse Creek, near Dubois, Wyoming. Bill tried to enlist in the army to fight the Kaiser, but explained, "The sons a bitches thought I was handicapped with this hand, little they knew about it!" Of working on his homestead, Bill would say, "Ya couldn't raise hell on it with a 50-gallon barrel of whiskey!" He worked on the cattle and dude ranches, and for the big game outfitters in the area to make a living.

The Daniels brothers also did some trapping, mostly for marten, but also for fox and coyote, the furs bringing the most money at the time. Like quite a number of other trappers back then, the brothers spent the winters many

Teton backcountry. Photo: Dave Bragonier

miles back in the mountains, running their trap-lines on snowshoes and skis. The trappers would supply their small cabins, situated ten to 15 miles apart, by packhorses in the fall of the year before the mountains were snowed-in. Back then, beaver were protected and had been ever since the relentless killing of the animals for their pelts almost wiped them out during the 19th century.

Without my ever daring to ask, Bill finally told me how he had lost his fingers. At the age of nine, he had been holding a block of firewood while his brother chopped with an ax! The little finger that remained had necessarily developed and Bill had no trouble whatsoever hoisting the panniers on the packhorses, swinging an ax, or doing any other task as far as I could tell.

Bill Daniels' most prized possessions were his four horses. And he was an excellent horseman, using a firm, but gentle, hand when working around them. His top saddle horse was a 1200-pound bay Morgan gelding named Red Cloud. The horse was 25 years old when I came upon the scene, and still going strong. Bill's other horses were Cheyenne, Joe, and Sailor (the horse I usually rode when working with Bill), all geldings. He always said that having mares in a string was inviting trouble. He said, "Mares, like women, should be kept busy, off the mountain, raisin' youngsters."

The old cowboy straddled an ancient, single-rigged, Heiser saddle and together with Forest Service packsaddles, he used his own two old Deckers, made by that same Denver saddler, upon which he slung two sets of time-worn cowhide panniers.

In addition to Bill's horses, we usually took along two or three government pack mules when leaving for the hills. The majority of the time, we tied the two-man diamond hitch on the packs. On a large top-pack, the double-diamond was thrown.

I soon learned that Bill had a deep appreciation for the environment, and this before the Great Movement! He knew that, somehow, all natural things are interconnected and important, and he would make interesting observations as we rode along the trail. This crusty old-timer actually kept notes of any interesting natural occurrence he witnessed. He sometimes made sketches of various flora, particularly the wildflowers to which he was partial, and noted where each specimen had been found. Bill respected all living things and would preach their significance.

We managed to spend as much time as possible at Bill's favorite place on earth: Hawks Rest. Near Bridger Lake and at the base of the mountain for which was named, the log building was strategically located on the east edge of the beautiful Yellowstone Meadows where several major trails crossed. Daniels and another old-timer, Pete Feuz, had built the cabin dur-

Bill Daniels at Hawks Rest Forest Service patrol station in the Teton Wilderness, 1956. Photo: Dave Bragonier

ing the hard times of World War II. Bill always said that he and Pete had to furnish the nails as the Forest Service couldn't (or wouldn't) come up with the money for them, along with many other items needed to build the structure. No wonder Bill was so possessive of that cabin!

For 20 years Bill spent much of each season stationed at Hawks Rest, and he was well known by many wilderness travelers, both backpackers and horsebackers, for his hospitality, respected advice, great knowledge of the area, and assistance during emergencies. The latter was very important as this location was many miles from the nearest road at Turpin Meadows on the Buffalo River.

Prior to the mid-50's when the Forest Service started using VHF two-way radios for communicating in the back-country, the government maintained a telephone line from Blackrock Ranger Station to Hawks Rest. From there, the phone line continued north into Yellowstone Park and the Thorofare Ranger Station, then down the Yellowstone River to the lake, down the east shore of Yellowstone Lake to the Sylvan Pass-East Entrance Road and on to Lake Ranger Station. In all, this phone line traversed over 60 miles of roadless country. Of course, it was a continuous task to keep this line in operation because of the blow-downs and other unpredictable occurrences in this mountainous region. One of Bill and Pete's summer and fall duties during the "telephone era" was maintaining the section of the line which crossed the Teton Forest, usually a full-time job.

By the time I arrived on the scene, the radio had come into play, but it was a far cry from modern technology, and many transmissions were so scratchy and faded that they were inaudible. Prior to The Wilderness Act of 1964, cabins, phone lines and chainsaws were not prohibited in "primitive areas."[1] Back then (as now), if a life-threatening emergency arose, an air rescue could be allowed by the forest supervisor. And, as is still the case, some people abuse this privilege.

One morning a horseman galloped up to the front door of the Hawks Rest patrol cabin. The anxious rider, a fishing outfitter, exclaimed that he had a guest at his Bridger Lake camp whom he feared was gravely ill. He believed the guest was dying of appendicitis. He asked us to obtain permission for an air evacuation for the dude. Bill called Blackrock and relayed the request for an air rescue. Within an hour, forest supervisor "Rip" Van Winkle had granted it.

Back then, though, there were only a few high-altitude helicopters stationed in the region, and none was available for the emergency. Dick Miller, a Wyoming Game and Fish Department pilot, happened to be at the Jackson Airport at the time. Miller, well known in the area for his ability as a mountain pilot, courageously offered his services to try to land his Super Cub somewhere in the area and airlift the dying man to the front country. As it seemed the only alternative, the valiant offer was considered. Van Winkle asked Daniels if he knew of a level area in the proximity of Bridger Lake that could be used as an emergency landing strip. Bill thought that it might be possible to use an area on the west side of the Yellowstone River, and just south of the mouth of Falcon Creek. This area was about a half mile from the outfitter camp, and a couple of miles from our location. Permission was granted to allow for the dangerous rescue attempt.

Bill and I left immediately for the location, and, with help from the outfitter's crew, we proceeded to remove rocks and brush - and flag the boulders that we couldn't budge - from the most level spot available. An emergency landing strip was prepared as well as time allowed, but we all agreed that a safe landing of a fixed-wing aircraft here would be dangerous even for a pilot of Miller's ability.

Within minutes Miller was above us, scouting out the strip. After a few

---

[1] Today's wilderness travelers in the area may wonder about the occasional insulator that can still be observed on a tree along the trail. While most of the old wire has now been removed, a coil of the stuff can still sometimes be found beside the trail by a startled horse and rider, or by an antlered animal that gets entangled in it. A moose head, with several wraps of the wire around it, hangs on the front of the game and fish Thorofare patrol cabin, attesting to a cruel death caused by the old line.

passes, and without hesitation, he brought the Cub to a bouncing stop on the ground next to us. We immediately loaded the patient into the cramped back seat of the little plane, and after using every inch of the makeshift airstrip, they were soon airborne!

We were amazed by what we learned later about the rescue. Supervisor Van Winkle and a group from town were gathered next to the ambulance waiting at the airport when Miller taxied his aircraft to a stop next to them. The onlookers were flabbergasted as the "dying fisherman" for whom Miller had risked his life leaped from the plane, hailed a taxi, and left for town! They overheard him say, "My ass is sore from the horseback ride into those damned mountains. And I wasn't about to ride a horse back out!"

This was probably the first, and hopefully the last, fixed-wing aircraft to land in the Yellowstone Meadows. Sadly, it will not be the last time that someone will show his blatant and selfish disregard for others.

Bill showed me the beautiful backcountry to the south of Yellowstone Park; from Deer Creek and Ishawooa Passes; to Wolverine Creek and Wildcat Ridge; and from Fox Park to the Buffalo Forks. He knew every inch of this Teton Wilderness.

As is still the case, the streams were naturally well stocked with Wyoming's only native trout, the cutthroat. The Continental Divide splits this vast wilderness, with the headwaters of the Yellowstone River to the east, and the headwaters of the Snake to the west. We had fish for supper often, and sometimes for breakfast. I caught them, and Bill cooked them. You bet they're good eating! And by the way, in the mountains, the cook never washes the dishes if someone else is in camp!

Daniels was an accomplished wildlife photographer, using both still and movie cameras. Many of his photographs can be seen in copies of *Wyoming Wildlife* from the '30s and '40s. Bill was also a self-taught artist, with a little advice and help from his good friend Joe Back. He used mostly oils, and the majority of his works were of big game animals and mountain scenes. Many of his elk paintings were unusual because they portrayed animals wounded by hunters. Bill had a great affection for animals, and when asked why he portrayed the elk suffering, he would say, "I've seen way too damn many elk crippled by hunters. And I paint it like it is!" For many years, several of Bill's paintings were displayed at the Jackson Game and Fish office.

Over the years, as he worked in this wilderness, Bill found that mistakes had been made on the existing maps of the area. Some drainages had been improperly positioned on the maps, while others were misnamed. He petitioned the U.S. Forest Service and the U.S. Geological Survey to correct the mistakes. And while he was at it, he suggested names for other, yet nameless locations. He named Weasel Creek on the Mink Creek drainage, and Thunder Mountain on the head of the Yellowstone River. Daniels Creek at Two Ocean Pass is named in Bill's deserving honor.

Bill retired from the Forest Service in 1960 at about 65 years of age. At the same time, the Wyoming Game and Fish department decided to discontinue the Blackrock elk feedground. By then, the feedground had attracted more moose than elk. Game officials felt that the 100 or so elk could spend future winters grazing on nearby Rosie's Ridge, and the moose would be much better off browsing the nearby Buffalo River willow bottoms. So the feedground retired with Bill.

This old ranger would have a profound and lasting influence on me. He had great respect for everything natural and knew that Nature's bounties should be used, but not abused. I am forever grateful for these early lessons.

Bill spent most of his remaining years on the Turner family's Triangle X Ranch. Jilted by his fianceé, a Riverton girl, when he was 19, he remained a confirmed bachelor from then on.

Thornton William "Bill" Daniels passed away on June 14, 1974. His ashes were returned to the mountains that knew him so well.

Evy—

It was so thoughtful of you to put this in front of me. I read and enjoyed it. I have driven through Yellowstone, the Tetons, and from Cody, WY, to the east entrance so I could visualize the area that he moves through. He is obviously committed to the protection of the outdoors, the animals, and idea of hunting but ethical hunting with fairness to all involved. I noted that early in the book he mentions that he is an Iowa State grad. It is humorous in places because he has no trouble using strong words, name-calling, in referring to those who use the outdoors and its life illegally. Thank you for sharing.

[signature] 9.27.2015

Gene

The Beginning of a Career

One late-summer evening, district game warden Dale West stopped by Blackrock ranger Station. Bill Daniels had introduced me to the warden several months earlier. West asked if I might be interested in working as a temporary special-deputy game warden to help patrol his north-Jackson warden district during the upcoming big game hunting season. Of course I was interested!

My total training for the job consisted of a ride through the hunting camps on Pacific Creek with Dale that first morning of the season. After being issued a red shirt (the Wyoming game warden's uniform shirt), a large silver badge and an old military Dodge Power Wagon, I was on my own.

The hunting season ran from September 10 through November, and things really got hectic when elk start migrating south out of Yellowstone Park and many hunters seemed to go berserk. Nearly 5,000 elk (and many moose and mule deer) were harvested in the Jackson Hole management unit that fall. Although it was a very busy season, I enjoyed the new experience.

That winter the department kept me on the payroll to feed elk in the Gros Ventre River country where the state operates three feedgrounds. I was to feed all three grounds: at Alkali Creek, on Fish Creek and at the Game and Fish patrol cabin where I would stay.

A brief history of Jackson Hole and its famous elk herds is probably in order here to explain why elk are fed in the area.

Jackson Hole is part of the wildlife-rich Yellowstone ecosystem where great herds of elk have summered for millennia. Because deep snow denies use of the area's lush mountain meadows during most winters, the vast herds historically migrated to lower elevations – before the arrival of white settlers there – to spend the winter where forage was easier to come by. One ancient elk migration route to and from the area crossed the hydrographic divide between the Gros Ventre River drainage and the Green River watershed where the once heavily used old trails can still be seen. Elk herds using this route would winter in the Green River Basin and on the Red Desert.

Beginning in the 1880s the ranching industry began to take over most of the elk herds' ancestral winter ranges. Although a few hundred elk continued to make the trek as late as 1911, the agricultural development of the Green River region prevented large herds from using the route. Constant market and subsistence hunting of elk on their desired winter ranges helped put an end to the animal's primordial migration routes. The elk herds would thereafter remain within the relative safety of Jackson Hole during the winter months where they would attempt to eke out an existence in open pockets and on wind-swept ridges.

The settlement of Jackson Hole made the great herd's survival even more precarious. During the winter of 1908, state game warden Dan Nowlin investigated reported congestion of elk in and near those settlements. The next year an estimated 20,000 to 30,000 elk wintered in Jackson Hole. The winter was a severe one and the settlers fed the animals what little hay they could spare. Still, thousands of elk died of starvation. Word of the dilemma reached Washington.

In 1913, Congress appropriated $50,000 to purchase land on which to raise hay for winter feeding. That year the National Elk Refuge was established on 1,040 acres set aside by executive order. From January 12 to March 27, 1916, 1,000 tons of hay was fed to 8,000 head of elk. The refuge was enlarged in 1927 by a gift of 1,700 acres of land purchased and donated by the Izaak Walton League. And by 1935 the game department had established several state feed grounds.

Of the 17,924 elk counted in Jackson Hole during the winter of 1956, 86 percent were on artificial feed at the federal refuge and state feedgrounds.[1]

Horse and mule teams are used to pull haysleds during elk-feeding operations. Snowshoes, skis and snowmobiles are used to access the more remote feed-sites.

Shortly before Christmas, Nick, my black Lab, and I piled into a J-5 Bombardier snowmachine for the journey up the 25 miles of snow-road to the Gros Ventre cabin to spend the winter. I had taken the horses and supplies – including an elk I had harvested for meat during hunting season – to the winter quarters, earlier, before the road had snowed-in.

My closest neighbor lived 15 miles down the valley at Lower Slide Lake. To the south, it was nearly 40 miles to an occupied residence on the upper Green River above Pinedale.

---

[1] The debate continues regarding the controversial practice of artificially feeding these elk. Animal congestion on feedgrounds creates unhealthy situations where disease and parasites such as brucellosis and scabies can more easily infect the herds. However, without feedgrounds the area's elk herds would be reduced dramatically. Locations in and near Jackson Hole are the only areas in the state where big game animals are artificially fed as a practice.

Wild Journey

Bull elk remains next to a secured private haystack in Jackson Hole, Wyoming. Photo: Dave Bragonier

The Alkali Creek feedground is situated six miles down the Gros Ventre (meaning "big belly" in French-Indian) River from the cabin, and Fish Creek feedground is located seven miles up the river from the station. Hay barns are located at each feedground. The procedure was to feed the 600 plus head of elk at Alkali one day and the 700 or so elk at Fish Creek the next, scattering out enough hay to last the animals two days. The 150 elk and two dozen moose at the cabin grounds were fed every evening.

The route down to Alkali Creek was rather hazardous because it had numerous windswept cutbanks where snowdrifts had to be continuously shoveled out (at times, both coming and going) to prevent tipping the 3200-pound Bombardier over the side of the road and straight down a hundred or more feet in places. Once, during a white-out, I did tip the heavy snowmobile on its side, where it teetered on the very edge of the road at a sheer cliff while Nick and I clambered safely out of the cab. Our luck wasn't entirely bad! As I stood in the raging blizzard collecting my thoughts before starting on the five-mile snowshoe trip back to the cabin, I spied a seemingly amused coyote watching the spectacle from a nearby knoll.

It took every daylight hour of a short winter day for travel and feeding at two locations. Usually it was early to bed, with coyotes often singing me a lullaby as moose munched willows outside the cabin window.

Dale West and area supervisor Ken Martin would usually come up once each month with mail and supplies. Folks seldom ventured far from plowed roads back then. The white wilderness was still peaceful, tranquil and free of obnoxious smells and noises. But the day of the recreation snow-scooter was fast approaching.

Permanent elk traps had been constructed at Alkali Creek and Fish Creek. Occasionally, during the mail runs when sufficient help was available, the traps were baited with hay and elk were captured, ear-tagged, fit with color-coded neck-bands and blood samples were taken from the animals. These procedures helped game managers learn more about both the herd's migration patterns and its health.

Around the first part of April, when the hills were beginning to bare of snow, I came out of the mountains.

The department placed me on permanent status that spring and trapping damage beaver became one of my duties. Beaver seem to enjoy damming culverts and irrigation ditches, flooding roads and buildings, and cutting

Moose fighting over hay at Wyoming Game and Fish Department Gros Ventre patrol cabin and elk feedground. Photo: Dave Bragonier

down trees just to keep in practice. At such times the animals were removed from an area, by live-trapping when adequate habitat was available for their relocation. For three years I patrolled the countryside for game violators, and trapped problem beaver during the summer and fall, and fed elk in the wintertime. There is worse duty than this!

After taking a competitive game warden examination, I was assigned a district of my own.

The Taxidermist's Friends

Each fall, when the elk are migrating to their winter range on the National Elk Refuge, slob hunters attempt to take the animals by any means available to them, day or night. At such times, game wardens come from around the state to help ride herd on these unethical nimrods.

One of the wardens who often assisted with this problem was Jim Arnoldi, then stationed at Kemmerer. Because the "spotlighters" (hunters who illegally kill wildlife with the aid of an artificial light) had begun their disgusting work, Jim and I were assigned to night patrol in the Antelope Flat area. Although elk hunting was then open in other parts of Grand Teton National Park and on Teton National Forest, the area we would be patrolling was closed to hunting to allow the elk an unrestricted corridor to their winter range on the refuge. And, of course, hunting big game animals at night is prohibited even in the open areas.

When Grand Teton National Park was established back in the 1920s, the state retained certain game management rights on those lands. Elk management in the park, including hunting, is a joint endeavor between state and federal agencies.

Late one night, Arnoldi and I had finished patrolling the Mormon Row-Ditch Creek areas and had begun working towards the Moran-Jackson highway. About midnight we stationed ourselves on a hill where we had a good view of traffic on the main highway.

After about an hour, a slow-moving vehicle appeared on the highway. It became apparent that something was up when the vehicle began stopping frequently. The vehicle finally came to a stop and the lights went out. Soon, flashlights were observed leaving the vehicle. No other vehicles or lights could be seen in the area.

Because we had heard no shots, we speculated that the game – most likely an elk – had been killed earlier, and now the poachers had returned to retrieve it. With the aid of the pickup's blackout light we moved from the hill closer to the highway so that we would be in a better position to both scrutinize the activity, and to apprehend the poachers when they left the area.

Wild Journey

We positioned ourselves about 100 yards from the highway and approximately a quarter-mile from the suspects' vehicle. The activity – most likely the butchering of elk – could be tracked by the flashlights. During the next hour, the suspects made several trips to the vehicle from two different locations on the sagebrush flat west the highway. Except for the howling of an occasional coyote, nothing could be heard in the cold, dark night as we silently waited.

About 2:00 a.m., the flashlights went out and the vehicle headed for town. We had inched our way to the highway and were now waiting there with our lights on – both headlights and reds – as the accelerating sedan rolled right on by.

We lurched onto the pavement behind them with tires squealing. With red lights running and siren screaming Jim gave the old pickup all it had, trying to keep up with the speeding poachers. The outlaws quickly out-distanced us as they sped towards town. All that we could tell for sure is the car was a dark-colored sedan with Wyoming plates. We were trailing a good mile behind as they crossed the Flat Creek Bridge and entered Jackson. The poachers turned right on one of the streets in the north end of town.

All seemed quiet in the small community by the time we arrived. In a grid pattern, we began to search the sleeping neighborhood where we suspected the car had entered. Not a light shown through a window, nor was there any activity to indicate the suspects' location. It soon became apparent that a little luck would be needed if we were to apprehend the poachers. Our good fortune, in the form of the poachers' carelessness, was soon to unfold.

Convinced that we were in the right neighborhood, our search continued there. Then, in the driveway of a residence, darned if there wasn't a car with its dome-light on! No other sign of life was apparent in the vicinity. We immediately pulled in behind the dark-colored sedan bearing Natrona County (Casper) license plates. In their great haste to get out of the car, someone had failed to close the door. On the ground at the passenger's side of the vehicle was a bloody rag, still steaming in the frigid night air. Looking into the car, we could see bloody chunks of meat on the floorboard of the back seat. The poachers had been located!

After considerable knocking on the door of the darkened abode, someone finally turned on the porch-light and came out yawning. It was a young taxidermist from the South who had set up shop in Jackson several months before. He recognized me and exclaimed in his Georgia accent, "Davey, what the hell brings you out at this time of night?" He was told that we wished to visit with the folks who had just arrived in the car, and asked him if he had been one of them. The taxidermist said that although he had not been with them, his house guests from Casper had just returned from a hunting trip and he yelled for them to come to the door.

Presently, three young men came out of the house. Two of them were in their early twenties and the other appeared to be a teenager. All three had blood stains on their hands. One of the older men – a large fellow with a big nose – took on the responsibility of spokesman for the group while the other two remained silent. He told us they had been hunting in the Flagg Ranch area where an elk had been shot. According to him, the animal had been killed quite a distance back from the road and they had worked late into the night packing the meat out. Cursing, the obnoxious spokesman said they had been sound asleep until we woke them up, and asked why we weren't out catching real poachers instead of bothering honest hunters in the middle of the night!

We asked to inspect the elk and check their licenses. Four quarters of elk meat and a set of antlers were found in the trunk. While all three of them had elk licenses, nobody had tagged the bull. The loud-mouthed one finally admitted to shooting the elk and said that he had just forgotten to tag it. This guy had a great vocabulary, and even Jim and I learned some new four-letter words from him.

Examining the quarters of meat, Jim exclaimed, "Hey, you guys killed an elk with two right shoulders!" This discovery was good news because we had nothing positive yet to tie them directly to the crime scene other than a rather vague vehicle description. Now, however, we knew where we would likely find another dead elk and it would have two left shoulders! After Jim's comment, even the foul-mouthed bandit clammed up.

The Flagg Ranch vicinity was open to elk hunting, and the hunters had probably been in that area earlier in the day. The elk were most likely shot on Antelope Flat as the hunters were returning to town about dark. The poachers had returned later that night to retrieve the meat and the chase had followed.

We had the Teton County Sheriff's office contact Ernie Wampler, one of the game wardens stationed in Jackson, to assist us with the search of the crime scene north of town. A sheriff's deputy remained at the taxidermist's residence to keep an eye on the suspects, and we headed back toward Antelope Flat.

It did not take long for us to locate where the poachers had left the parked car. A white handkerchief had been tied to a sagebrush, apparently to mark the location. The bloody drag-trail in the snow confirmed our suspicions. About 200 yards west of the road we found the kill-sites of two elk, and four elk quarters, two of which were left-front quarters.

Upon returning to Jackson, we were not surprised to find that all the elk quarters matched up perfectly. The county put the poachers up for the rest of the night to ensure their appearance in court. The two older fellows wished to take full responsibility for the incident. Although the teenager had assisted in the illegal acts – and was certainly old enough to know better – he would not be charged.

Since the violations had occurred in Grand Teton National Park, the poachers could be charged in either state or federal court. Because penalties for game violations are usually more severe at the federal level, we contacted park ranger Doug McLarin and arranged to take the offenders to the federal magistrate's court in Jackson.

The elk slayers were taken in front of the magistrate for killing the two elk in an area of the park that was closed to hunting. The obscene individual pleaded guilty to shooting both elk. He told the judge that they had intended to go back after the other quarters of meat later. The poacher had to pay $300, a hefty fine by 1960 standards.

Years later I ran into the taxidermist in a Casper restaurant. He had long since moved his business to that city. I hadn't seen him since the incident, and he still denied any implication in the poaching activities that night long ago.

He asked if I remembered the names of the game violators who were involved in the incident. It was no secret that the obscene poacher had afterwards been hired as a biologist for the Wyoming Game and Fish Department and was later promoted to a much higher position. However, I did not realize until then that the teen-aged poacher – continuing in the footsteps of his mentor – had also later become a biologist for the department.

Little Snake River Tales

Tom Vernon
Remembers Butch Cassidy

My first full-fledged warden assignment was at the newly established Baggs warden district, and just in time for the hunting season. One can imagine how busy and confused I was as I performed my game warden duties that first season in a country yet unfamiliar to me. To say my first two months in this Little Snake River Valley country that straddles the Wyoming-Colorado state line were hectic would be putting it mildly.

While the district is a large one, consisting of both mountains and desert with large and diverse wildlife populations, its occupancy by humans (including the towns of Baggs, Dixon and Savory) is considerably fewer than 1,000 inhabitants, a figure which has varied little over the last 100 years. However, the region has an interesting history.

Tom Vernon, proprietor of the valley's only hotel, was one of the first people I met after my arrival in town. I became better acquainted with Tom after things slowed down that fall.

Well into his eighties at the time, Tom had spent most of his adult life in the valley. When a lad of 18, he had left his home state of Missouri for the West shortly before the turn of the century. The young man ended his westward trek in the yet-raw Little Snake River country where he found work as a ranchhand.

Young Vernon was fascinated by the ruggedness of both the land and the area's residents. He was especially interested in the frequent visitors from Powder Wash a few miles to the west: Butch Cassidy's Wild Bunch.

On his way to the valley, Tom had stopped for a while in Steamboat Springs and while there acquired a violin made in that town.[1] Vernon told of playing the fiddle at dances held whenever the outlaws came to town, and remembered that Butch would often pitch a silver dollar his way as the outlaw danced by with a gal in his arms.

---

[1] Tom Vernon allowed the author to examine the old violin. The maker's name, town and date of construction (1888) could be seen on an inside label in green ink through the hole under the strings.

Local folks were well acquainted with the gang's reputation, but, since the good-natured outlaws were very generous to the residents and never committed atrocities in the valley, they were generally welcome there.

Chuckling as he told the story, Tom related an incident involving Cassidy that had occurred at the Dixon stage station five miles up the river from Baggs.

A young man had recently arrived in the valley from the east coast and was employed as a bartender at the stage stop. The local yokels had primed the easterner by telling him about the "fearsome" outlaws who frequented the area and how they would shoot anyone who wasn't fast enough to get out of their way. The greenhorn bartender soon began to dread the day he was sure to bump into Butch, the Sundance Kid, Kid Curry or one of the others. It was said that he often prayed he would never run into the entire bunch all at once!

That day finally came, however, when the outlaw gang rode in from Brown's Hole and tied their horses to the stagestop's hitchrail. Inside the saloon, the announcement of the Wild Bunch's arrival was made, and out front the locals were hastily filling the outlaws in on the fine details of the hijinks. Upon entering the saloon, the wayward cowboys unholstered their guns and began waving them about menacingly. To everyone's delight, it was quite apparent that the easterner was petrified with fear!

After a while, Cassidy sidled up behind the bar next to the dude bartender who was nervously serving drinks to the smelly horsemen. The bartender, though aware of Butch's presence, refused to glance his way and was trying his dangedest to ignore the outlaw leader. When the tension seemed at an appropriate level, Butch stuck the barrel of his .45 in a half-full slopbucket next to the dude and touched off a round.

The gunshot's concussion launched a great gush of the bucket's contents skyward and drenched both outlaw and barkeep with equal application. The duped tenderfoot sprang over the bar, shot through the door, and was last observed heading in an easterly direction at a full gallop!

The successful pranksters rolled on the saloon's floor and on the ground outside in severe throes of glee. The story was repeated around many campfires and bar tables for years to come.

While sitting in the lobby of the old Vernon Hotel discussing the possible demise of the outlaws, I asked Tom if he thought Cassidy and Sundance had been killed in Bolivia as most authorities claim. Without the least hesitation the elderly gentleman exclaimed that he knew Cassidy had survived his escapades in South America because Butch and three other men had driven up to the hotel in a Ford car a number of years back. They spent a short time in the area and then drove off to the north. Vernon, having visited with him, knew the driver of the car to be Cassidy without question. He said, "Although Butch's hair had turned white, I could still recognize those eyes and that lantern jaw!"

Since the stories connected with these infamous outlaws and their uncertain demise had long fascinated me, I pressed Tom for a more precise time when the four men had made their appearance in the Baggs community. He immediately yelled to his wife who was in the other room and had not been party to our conversation, asking her, "Was that just before or after the Second World War when Butch Cassidy stopped by here?" She yelled right back, "It was just before the war!"

The impromptu conversation about Butch Cassidy between the two old-timers who knew him – and who had nothing whatsoever to gain or lose by telling it – suggests that the outlaw survived well into the 20th century.

Sedgwick County's Finest

Before the establishment of the Baggs game warden district, hunters came to know that the Little Snake River region was not frequently patrolled for game violators. Many nimrods, resident and non-resident alike, took advantage of this lack of game law enforcement. Included among these unethical hunters was a group, led by a Kansas sheriff, that came to the area annually. That there was now a game warden stationed in the region was not welcome news around some campfires.

In the early 60's, Wyoming's mule deer herds were burgeoning and producing some monstrous bucks. To keep on top of the herd, the game department had set a three-deer bag limit season in the area. A liberal season such as this one, while appearing to cheapen the resource, is sometimes necessary to balance game animals with their habitat.

The November mule deer hunt was popular with hunters not only because it was so liberal, but also because it corresponded with the start of the rut which make the bucks lose their usual wariness. The area has long been a favorite with Kansas hunters for whom the trip to southern Wyoming usually only takes about a day.

Many of the deer harvested that day were taken in an unsportsmanlike manner, and a number of tickets had been written by dark. Citations were issued for violations ranging from "trespassing to hunt on private lands" and "shooting from a public road" to "failing to properly tag a deer." Too many hunters lose all common sense in the heat of the hunt. Some folks call it buck fever.

Most game wardens are tickled to death when the sun sets on the first day of hunting season. This certainly held true on that opening day of the Baggs multiple deer season. Wyoming hunters can legally shoot until an hour after sundown. However, a game warden's day rarely stops at dark during hunting seasons and this day would be no exception.

Wyoming is no different from many other states when it comes to the slob-hunting spotlighters (called jacklighters in the East). Spotlighters are the really bad apples who would rather cheat even when hunting is terrific and there is no need to be unethical to harvest game.

It had been dark about an hour and I was halfway through supper when the phone rang off the hook. The caller was a Savory rancher who told me that some hunters had stopped on the highway and shot directly toward his ranchhouse while using a spotlight. He didn't know if the spotlighters had killed any deer, but said that at dark there had been a herd of the animals in the general area of the hayfield where the shooting had occurred. The rancher had jumped in his truck and caught up with the spotlighters as they headed west towards Baggs. The suspect vehicle was a light brown Chevy pickup with a camper on it with the words "Sedgwick County Sheriff's Posse" on the side of the pickup. While the landowner didn't get the vehicle license number, he observed that it was a Kansas plate.

In my pickup, I headed east on the Savory-Baggs highway that runs directly in front of the warden station. Within a mile I met the vehicle in question, turned around, and then stopped it.

Walking up to the driver's side with my flashlight, I could see that the passenger was holding a rifle between his legs. Another gun in a case was leaning against the seat between the two occupants of the vehicle. Wyoming is one of a mere handful of states where it is not illegal to have an assembled and uncased gun in a vehicle. It is, however, illegal to shoot from, across or along a public road or highway. As I began questioning them about the rancher's complaint, the driver immediately exclaimed, "You should know that I'm the sheriff of Sedgwick County, Kansas – here's my card – and this here's my sergeant. We certainly wouldn't do anything like what you're describing. The rancher is mistaken. We're sworn to uphold the law. There was another pickup camper just behind us – I'll bet that's it – that's the one you want, and that farmer is confused. We didn't drive all the way out here, and spend all that money for those expensive licenses of yours, and everything else, just to get in trouble – no-siree!"

By the description given me, I felt sure this was the right outfit and asked if it would be all right to look around. The high sheriff said that he had no problem with me looking around as they had nothing to hide, but said, "Make it quick, we're hungrier 'n bears and heading to town to get something to eat." The hunters said they made a late start from Kansas and had just arrived in the area about dark so they hadn't hunted yet.

While looking things over, I shined my light towards the top of the camper and noticed something that appeared to be a liver lying on the edge of the camper-top. Holding my light on it, I asked them what it was. The sergeant exclaimed, "Oh, that's a deer liver. I forgot to take it off. I guess I did get a doe just before dark."

Earlier, I had asked to look at their deer licenses and still had them in my hand. I could see that the sergeant had not tagged the deer. He said the deer was back at camp, and that he had just forgotten to tag it. According to both of them, it was an honest mistake. I told them their supper would have to wait for now as I wanted to see the deer. So far, nothing they had said sounded truthful, and I now began to doubt if they were really hungry.

They led me several miles to their camp which consisted of another pickup camper, a trailer and a tent. Other "posse" members were scurrying around the site. The deer in question was stashed way back in the trees out of sight and was most likely going to be their "camp meat."

As I wrote the sergeant a ticket for the tagging violation, the Kansas officers wondered aloud why I couldn't show them the same professional courtesy that I would be shown back in their state. The hunters seemed relieved, though, that this was the only violation they were being charged

Doe mule deer shot and abandoned by Kansas sheriff near Savory, Wyoming. Photo: Dave Bragonier

with. If they were in a relaxed mood now, it was fine with me, but there was more investigation to be done regarding the spotlighting incident at Savory. Of course, at the time I didn't know if an animal had been killed there or not. However, I had recorded the serial number of the .32 caliber Winchester rifle that the sergeant had been holding earlier in the evening. It had been a long day, and now, if nothing else came up, I was ready to get a fresh start in the morning.

Sunrise found me back at Savory where the spotlighting incident had occurred the night before. From the ranchhouse, the landowner pointed out the approximate location where the suspects had been shooting from the highway. I parked at the corner of the hayfield and began searching the ground for evidence along the west-bound lane of the highway. Concentrating on the area designated by the rancher, I soon found four empty .32 Winchester Special cartridge cases at the edge of the road. One was of Remington manufacture and the other three were Winchester cases. Found near the spent cases was a right-hand black leather glove with its owner's teeth-marks plainly visible on the finger-tips, most likely made at the time it was hastily removed to free a trigger finger for shooting.

On a straight line between the evidence along the road and the ranchhouse was a yearling doe mule deer carcass, lying in an irrigation ditch. The deer, after being shot, had either fallen or had been dragged into the ditch. No attempt had been made to salvage the animal's meat. It looked as if the bullet might still be in the carcass. Even though there was now enough evidence for an arrest, a positive ballistics test on a bullet that came from the Winchester rifle would clinch the case if it went to a jury.

As I began pulling the deer carcass to the road, the suspects' vehicle went by heading west. They had likely wanted to visit the crime scene to see what was going on. Their worst suspicions were probably confirmed! In a matter of seconds, the pickup sped back in the opposite direction and towards camp. It was apparent what the lawmen had in mind now: they were going to pull up stakes and boogie for Kansas!

After loading the deer carcass into the pickup, I was soon headed towards the Kansas hunting camp. The two poachers were wildly throwing things into their camper as I drove up. Some of the hunters had not yet come back from the field, but all hands in camp were frantically packing their bags. A cloud of dust actually hung over the camp.

I went directly to the cab of the sheriff's pickup truck. In plain view on the dash were two boxes of .32 Winchester Special ammunition, one each of Winchester and Remington. Next to them was a left-hand black leather glove, the mate to the one I had found at the crime scene.

The two lawmen were now told that they were looking at charges of killing a deer with the aid of a spotlight, wanton waste of a game animal and shooting from a public road. Sensing that I meant business, the crusty old sheriff tried intimidating me. He could tell that I was a nervous rookie and may have thought such a tactic might work. The seasoned law officer began by telling me that he had been in law enforcement for over 30 years, saying, "Kid, you had damn well better know what you're doing or there will be hell to pay. Have you ever heard of false arrest?" Answering his question affirmatively, I also let him know that even Wyoming law officers were given a little training. Sure I was nervous but my determination must have also showed a little.

The head law officer of Sedgwick County led his sergeant just out of earshot where they had an intense discussion.

After a while the Kansas cops came back over to me. The sheriff's demeanor had changed considerably. He now humbly presented a field plea-bargain to me. He told me that one of them might plead guilty to the game violations if I promised not to charge the other with being an accessory to the violations. Wyoming did not have an accessory statute pertaining to misdemeanor crimes at the time. Since the state could prosecute only the principal violator anyway, I accepted the arrangement.

The sheriff then painfully told me that he was the one who shot the deer and was ready to get the matter taken care of. Because the sergeant held the suspect rifle that night, I thought it more likely that he had shot the deer. On the other hand, they were really equally guilty of the offenses. The plea bargain was still fine with me.

When the Baggs justice of the peace, Mildred Jesmer, asked how he pleaded to the game violations, the sheriff replied, "I guess I'll have to plead guilty." The judge immediately exclaimed, "There will be no guess work in this court. Are you guilty or not guilty?" The whipped sheriff quickly replied, "Guilty, your honor!"

The defendant was fined $200, a stiff fine back then, and lost his hunting and fishing privileges in Wyoming for two years.

The sheriff and his entourage left immediately for Kansas with the not-so-fond memories of their Wyoming debacle.

The rest of the story gradually found its way back to Wyoming. Earlier in the year, the sheriff had decided not to run for re-election. The sergeant ran for the office and had been elected sheriff just before the hunting trip. The plea-bargain agreement was meant to protect the new sheriff.

So the sheriff-elect had been the triggerman and the old sheriff drove the get-a-way car.

Game Wardening
in the Big Horns

Punchin' Elk

At the end of 1962, game warden John Aeschbach retired, leaving the Little Horn district vacant in northern Sheridan County. I was selected to take over the warden duties there.

John owned a small, picturesque ranch on the state line at the confluence of the West Fork with the Little Bighorn River where he had lived for many years with his wife, Anna, together with a few cows and a dozen horses. As a boy he had begun riding the ranges of the southern Montana cow outfits. Aeschbach knew Indian sign language and could speak the Crow tongue fluently.

Game department officials had two major considerations in mind when the Little Horn game warden district was carved from the Dayton district in 1953. The department needed a warden who could ride herd on both the elk and the Indians. The game and fish department had just purchased land for an elk winter range in the Pass Creek-Little Horn area and had fenced its northern boundary. Warden Aeschbach had been the fence construction foreman for the project. Now, Sheridan County sportsmen were expecting an increase in the area's elk herds. In order for this to happen, though, the elk must be kept within their winter pasture and off private lands. Also, it would be necessary to keep a constant vigil on the "northern neighbors" so that poaching on the herds would be kept to a minimum. Although Aeschbach had gotten a rather late start at game wardening, he was the right man for the job.

For ten years Aeschbach did outstanding work in the warden district. Then the day for John to retire finally arrived. He had never produced a birth certificate, and many folks thought it likely the old range rider was in his 70's at the time. Still as hard as nails, John kept on breaking colts after retirement.

It had been an unusually harsh winter and at the time of my arrival in January, several feet of snow covered the Kerns elk pasture, which had been established to reduce competition between elk and livestock. Few of the pasture's one thousand residents remained within. Most of the animals were

Wild Journey

Game warden punchin' elk from private land onto the game department's Sheridan County game winter range. Photo: Wyoming Game and Fish Department

foraging on private lands at the lower elevations. A large number of elk had drifted across the state line onto the Crow Indian Reservation, never to return. Landowners were concerned that the elk were impacting their livestock operations. One rancher demanded that all elk be removed from his lands immediately. Just how this was to be accomplished mattered not to him.

As long as the thick blanket of snow covered the elk pasture's lush grass, there was nowhere to push the elk. All that could be done was to try to alleviate damage to the haystacks by fencing them and chasing the animals off. Finally, the chinook winds came and again exposed the grass on the ridges.

Upon Aeschbach's retirement, the warden district headquarters were moved back to Dayton. From there it was a 100-mile round-trip to John's old station on the Little Horn.

The big push to the Bighorn Mountain region was late in the settlement of Wyoming. While other areas within the territory had been thriving for years, it was not until the late 1800s that white settlers could safely come to the region, which had been named for the area's native sheep. Open winters and quality forage produced an abundance of game, and it's small wonder the Plains Indians fought tooth and nail to keep their hunting grounds for themselves. White settlement in the region began shortly after the 1876 Fight at the Little Bighorn. By 1920 little public land remained in the foothill areas on the east side of the Bighorns.

With an average annual precipitation close to 20 inches, and an elevation gamut ranging between 3500 to 6000 feet and considerably under the 7000-foot mean elevation of Wyoming, the foothills lie within a chinook belt and are blessed with mild winters.

Early settlers of Pass Creek country, in what is today northern Sheridan County, found a canyon bestrewn with "shed" elk antlers and they named it Elkhorn Canyon. It is known that elk originally ranged year-round in areas distant from the mountains. However, as settlement and ranching activity increased in these outlying areas, elk gradually ranged closer to the chinook belt in the mountain foothills.

By 1900, only small numbers of deer and elk populated the area. The Bighorn region soon mirrored other areas of the West. A general decline in big game populations was simultaneous with increasing settlement. Market hunting was common and the depredators slashed game herds to fragmentary numbers. Settlers, in need of meat, also took advantage of the region's vanishing game animals.

Conservation-minded ranchers and sportsmen in the Sheridan area set out to restore the elk herd in the Bighorns. Largely through their efforts, a transplant of 23 elk from Jackson Hole was made to the Eaton Ranch in 1910. Additional transplants of elk were made in the Dayton vicinity within the next few years. Transplanted elk drifted north and again became established in the Little Horn and Pass Creek drainages.

Elk increased in numbers and by the 1940's landowners became concerned with the wapiti rebirth. During the summer months, elk thrived in the mountains, but in the winter they moved down country to forage on low-lying private lands to compete with livestock for food. Periods of deep snow drove the elk farther north onto the Crow Indian Reservation where open hunting prevailed.

It soon became evident that something would have to be done to remove the range competition between elk and livestock. The Sheridan County Sportsmen's Association and other interested groups started the ball rolling. Land purchase negotiations began with the help of the Wyoming Game and Fish Commission and in January, 1950, with aid from federal funds, the commission purchased 4,411 acres from the Kerns Brothers. The Sheridan County Game Winter Range was then established. Locally it was known as the Kerns Elk Pasture.

This ideally located winter habitat is situated adjacent to the Bighorn National Forest. Elk calving grounds on the sagebrush benches of the Dry Fork drainage and adequate summer pasture throughout the area made the

Wild Journey

Elk moving along Sheridan County game winter range fence on the Kerns elk pasture. Photo : Wyoming Game and Fish Department

Kerns tract a promising winter elk refuge. The natural reserves in the road-less canyon areas afforded protection for elk during hunting seasons.

The purchase of the Kerns Pasture reduced elk use of private lands, and the county continues to receive tax money for the property, paid by the game and fish department.

Included within the Kerns Pasture were several hundred acres of previously irrigated lush grasslands located on Dana (TR) Bench. In the early days, homesteaders harvested wild hay from the area.

To discourage elk from moving north onto private lands bordering the Kerns Pasture, the game and fish department constructed an eight-foot fence in 1953. The installation also included construction of an access road into the pasture. Crossing three large canyons (Gay Creek, Red and Elkhorn Canyons), construction began at the west fork of Pass Creek and ended in the bottom of Kettle Gulch, covering a distance of nine miles. Since the fence is open-ended, to allow elk coming down from their summer ranges in the mountains access to the pasture, inlets were built into it at strategic locations to allow for the return of elk found outside on the private land.

Elk from adjacent areas were attracted to the Kerns unit and the band grew into one of the most reproductive and healthy herds in the state. The pasture now winters about 1000 head of elk. Once again, elk winter on their ancestral range and bulls shed their antlers in Elkhorn Canyon.

There are few winters when snow lies for more than a month at a time on the lower reaches of the range. Chinook winds generally warm the area and uncover forage for the game. With food usually available, winter mortality of elk in the area is low. Large scale artificial feeding of elk is seldom necessary in the Bighorn region. Rotational (seasonal) grazing by the elk allows the range to recover from previous grazing and adequately carries the herd when it returns the next winter.

Elk escape the pasture during inclement weather when they either cross over the eight-foot fence on snowdrifts, or go around the ends of it. There are also a few belligerent old cows around to lead other elk out of the pasture regardless of the weather conditions.

Once out of the Kerns Pasture, the elk must be put back into the unit by driving them either through the inlets or around the ends of the fence. Herding elk from private lands back onto the Kerns Elk Pasture was a full-time job many winter months during the 60's. Sometimes, where the country will allow, snowmachines can be used to drive the elk. In rough terrain, however, saddle horses become necessary. Horses are the most effective way to move elk without stressing them. During winter months wild animals can scarcely afford to expend energy racing up and down mountains with a motorized vehicle behind them.

In the early 1960s, the game and fish purchased another tract of land for a big game winter range at Amsden Creek. Without the district's two state-owned winter ranges, few elk would frequent the hills of northern Sheridan County today.

You Owe Us!

Wyoming game wardens have numerous encounters with Native American hunters. A number of these hunters have been convicted for violating the state's game laws. Game is scarce in accessible areas of both the Crow and the Wind River (Shoshoni-Arapaho) Indian Reservations due to over-harvest of that resource. Tribal hunters, who also call themselves game wardens, usually help with this herd reduction. Many of today's Indian hunters target managed herds off the reservation.

A myriad of big game animals had been poached during nighttime with aid of artificial light or "spotlighted" along Sheridan County's Pass Creek Road, between the Kerns elk pasture and the stateline Crow Indian Reservation boundary. Sections had been cut from the eight-foot-high pasture fence, which allowed elk to drift northward onto the reservation.

I had just arrived early one February morning with a horse to push elk off the Fuller Ranch and back into their pasture. As usual, before saddling up, I drove to a good vantage-point on a public access road barely inside the reservation to determine exactly where the herds were located so that I would ride up the proper ridge. I was glassing the country between Elkhorn Canyon and Kettle Gulch where at least 200 of the animals were grazing on Fuller Ranch land, when a Crow Indian drove up in a pickup and parked a short distance from my location.

The fellow, from my generation, sauntered over to me and asked if I knew I was standing on "Crow land." Before I could answer that question, he said, "I'm going up there," pointing into Wyoming, "and kill some of those elk!" Because he was safely within his reservation, the brazen Indian began toying with me.

I let him know there would be trouble if he killed an elk in Wyoming. Immediately upon hearing this, he exclaimed, "Don't you think that you Whites owe us?" I acknowledged to him that many injustices had undeniably been dealt Native Americans throughout our history. I told him, however, that I had a problem with taking the blame for all my forefathers' transgressions.

Wild Journey

I walked with the Indian back to his pickup to satisfy my curiosity. I had seen deer legs protruding above the truck's bed. The Indian had killed six mule deer, mostly does, somewhere the night before. The Crow hunter had actually killed more than six deer because at that time of year each mature doe would most likely be carrying twin fetuses.

Holding onto an old custom, many Native Americans kill deer and elk during late-winter and early-spring to procure the unborn fetuses which they consider culinary delicacies. Year-round American Indian hunting traditions affects off-reservation game management in many places around the country.

Folks should be allowed to practice their traditions as long as the laws and rights of others are not violated in the process. However, when such pursuits conflict with the legitimate interests of others, something's got to change. That is, unless one side or the other is willing to pull up stakes and clear completely out of the picture, which will never happen.[1]

The majority of humankind has learned out of necessity to modify its primordial "hunter/gatherer" traditions throughout the ages. Some Native Americans have it figured out.

Take for instance the Apache people of the Southwest. Through proper game management of reservation herds they are able to reap substantial revenues from those renewable wildlife resources and still keep alive certain valued tribal traditions within their reserves. The White Mountain, Jicarilla and Mescalero Apache Tribes, each on their own reservation, have established a national reputation for themselves among trophy hunters seeking record-class mule deer bucks and bull elk. Skilled tribal game managers oversee free-ranging big game herds that are the envy of many.

With the will, other Native Americans can do the same.

As I rode up the mountain that day, my thoughts kept drifting back to the encounter with the rather militant Native American and his "you owe me"

---

[1] In 1989, Wyoming game warden Chuck Repsis arrested Thomas Ten Bear, a Crow Indian, for killing an elk without a license on the Bighorn National Forest. Ten Bear was convicted of the offense in October of 1990. The Crow Tribe then filed a lawsuit against the State of Wyoming claiming that their members had "unrestricted hunting and fishing rights on unoccupied lands of the United States so long as game may be found thereon," given them by the 1868 Fort Laramie Treaty. In 1994, U.S. District Judge Alan B. Johnson dismissed the tribe's case based on the 1898 U.S. Supreme Court ruling in the Ward versus Race Horse case. In that famous case involving Chief Race Horse of the Bannock Tribe, the high court ruled that "the right conferred on the Indians by the treaty would be of no avail to justify a violation of the state law," and that such treaties are "temporary and precarious." The Crow Tribe appealed the ruling to the U.S. Supreme Court where it was upheld in May of 1996.

attitude. Because of my interest in American history I knew something about the Crow Tribe. I was also aware of the mysterious Medicine Wheel.

This curious prehistoric relic is located on the north side of Medicine Mountain in the Big Horn Mountains, at 9,642 feet above sea level. It is constructed of stones laid side by side, forming an almost perfect circle 70 feet in diameter. Around the rim of the wheel there are six small cairns, or monuments, about two and a half feet high. When the Medicine Wheel was first discovered by white men, the cairns were built up on three sides and the other side had been left open, after the fashion of an armchair. Five of them had the open side facing toward the center of the wheel, and the sixth, which is the one on the east, had the open side facing outward toward the rising sun.

The enigmatic Medicine Wheel always produces questions in the minds of observers. Photo: Bighorn National Forest

In the center of the wheel is a hub, 12 feet in diameter, and around the huge outer edge is a circular wall two and a half feet thick. This leaves an opening in the center seven feet in diameter. This was most likely used for some sacred purpose, but no evidence can be found which might explain the ceremonies performed within this structure. There are 28 spokes leading from the hub, or center monument, to the outer rim of the wheel. On the outside of the wheel, at distances of from 70 to 275 feet, other monuments are found, all built upon high points.

Authorities now believe the mysterious structure to be at least 7,500 years old. Despite current tribal claims to it, Crow Indian oral history handed down from one generation to the next by tribal elders tells that the "Medicine Wheel" atop the Big Horn Mountains was already there when the Crow people arrived.

The Crow and other American Indian tribes are now laying claim to the Medicine Wheel, first given protection by the White race, as a sacred religious site of their ancestors. Some would keep all others from entering the area. Strangely, during all this contentious oratory by some tribal members, another event was unfolding farther to the west.

In July of 1996, a half-buried human skeleton was found along the Columbia River near the town of Kennewick in southeastern Washington. The skeleton was that of a man, middle-aged at death, with Caucasian features, judging by skull measurements. Imbedded in his pelvis was a spearhead made of stone. Bone samples of "Kenniwick Man" were radio carbon dated at the University of California at Riverside and determined to be 9,200 years old.

In the world of old bones and educated conjecture about the first Americans, the Columbia River skeleton is a riveting discovery. It adds credence to the theories that some early inhabitants of North America came from European stock, perhaps migrating across northern Asia and into the western hemisphere over a land bridge exposed in the Bering Sea about 12,000 years ago, or earlier, near the end of the last Ice Age.

The bones, one of the best preserved and oldest skeletons ever found in North America, are causing a modern rift over matters of race and ancient ties to the land. The find means that some of our ideas about prehistory may need to be revised.

Although some American Indians have been demanding that Kenniwick Man be turned over to them for reburial, anthropologists say a discovery of such enormous importance merits a bit more time for study.

"This is a battle over who controls America's past," commented Dr. Robson Bonnichsen, director of the Center for the Study of the First Americans at Oregon State University. "We have always used the term paleo-Indian to describe the remains of this era. But this may be the wrong term. Maybe some of these guys were really just paleo-American."

Might Kenniwick Man have built the rock structure in the Big Horn Mountains before others drove the ancients from their land?

A Stacked Deck

The day was breaking cold, clear and calm over a snowy landscape, ideal conditions for an aerial game count. I had just arrived at the Sheridan County Airport that January morning to begin annual trend counts of the Dayton warden district's elk herds. The count is a good indicator of whether the elk population is on an upward or downward trend.

In that country, though, perfect wintertime flying conditions are rare. Chinook winds usually come on the heels of a snowstorm and the warm zephyrs can peel two feet of snow from the foothills in a matter of hours. Most of the Big Horn Mountains' elk herds winter within this chinook belt.

Game department pilot Mel Clark soon had the Super Cub airborne and heading for the Tongue River Canyon game winter range. This winter habitat on the Bighorn National Forest, together with the two state units of Amsden Creek and Kerns Elk Pasture, is where the majority of elk would be found. Smaller herds winter at other locations along the face of the mountain north to Marble Quarry Ridge on the Montana state line.

It was approaching noon when we arrived over the Pass Creek drainage. The one hundred or so elk that normally winters near the forest boundary here, were bedded down for the day much higher up the mountain than usual. It was obvious that something had disturbed them at the lower elevations. Flying down their funnel-pattern back trail soon told the story. Three gut piles were seen fairly close together on the lands of two adjacent ranches. The elk probably had been shot at daybreak that morning. Two drag trails showed where the poachers had used horses to pull the carcasses east to a county road. No sign of the perpetrators' vehicles or horses could now be seen on or near this road. Coincidental with our arrival was the presence of a county snowplow, busy clearing the road and at the same time obliterating all tracks from it. I swore at the outlaws' good fortune.

Tracks, both coming and going from the other direction, of a crawler-type tractor pulling a sled, ended at the third gut pile. Following these tracks west across private land we soon overtook a Caterpillar tractor pulling a hay sled with the elk on it. I recognized the elderly rancher when he waved at us and then continued on towards his ranch with the spoils. He was about a mile away from his ranch at the time and we knew that he would be there shortly. Wishing to be present at the ranch buildings upon the rancher's arrival there, I asked Mel what the chances were of his landing on a country road near the ranch buildings. After checking the road for traffic, and without further ado, the able pilot set the craft down and taxied to a stop near the ranchhouse.

After helping Mel turn the Cub around, I was soon hoofing it towards the buildings and the sound of the oncoming tractor. The pilot had agreed to return to the ranch with my state pickup.

The Cat was just behind the hill when I arrived at the ranchhouse. The rancher's son-in-law, upon seeing the plane land, came running from the house. He told me in no uncertain words to leave the ranch immediately. Walking rapidly towards the barn, I told him that I had business with his father-in-law. He knew why I was there, and therefore kept on threatening me. With the guy on my heels, I met the old-timer at the barn as he was shutting off the tractor.

He immediately exclaimed, "Warden, if ya know what's good for ya, you'll back on outa here. "Old so and so" (a former game warden in the area) caught me years ago, just 'bout like this, and he was smart 'nough ta leave without stirrin' the pot!" When I asked why he had to kill an elk two months after the season, he said, "I didn't kill it – but let me tell ya – the game n' fish better start thinkin' 'bout how they're gonna get all the elk and deer off this place – they're eatin' me outa house and home – both here'n up on ma guv'-ment lease on the forest. It's gettin' so ma cows don't have nothin' left ta eat when them sonsabitchin' elk get done! That's all I'm gonna say fer now, 'cept to recommend that you leave pronto!"

I wasn't surprised when no rifle was found on the tractor. The shooting had occurred hours before, and the vehicle had only been used to retrieve the elk. It may be that the rancher hadn't actually killed the elk, but it was obvious that he had driven directly to the kill site and received a share of the illegal proceeds.

The son-in-law, who had been silently skulking nearby, now chimed in with is father-in-law, "Yea, you get the hell outa here!" I replied that I would leave when the matter at hand was taken care of. The rancher was given several chances to offer any extenuating circumstances that might benefit him. He chose not to implicate anyone else, and told me to get on with my business.

Now I would wait for Clark to arrive with the pickup – and my citation book. The landowner left for the house with his son-in-law trailing behind him like a little puppy.

Game damage was not the real issue here. It was just a handy topic to mention at the moment. Wyoming's "Cowboy" Legislature has passed a series of liberal game damage laws, weighted heavily in favor of landowners. While there are times when landowners suffer game damage and should be compensated for it, many claims are unjustly filed. And all game damage complaints – frivolous or not – must be worked by game wardens. It is very likely that the seasoned cattleman had successfully used the threat of game damage on a previous warden as he claimed he had.

Mel finally arrived with the pickup and the rancher received a citation charging him with "illegal possession of an elk." As we were driving off, the wealthy old stockman yelled after us, "You'll need lotsa luck ta make this stick. And don't fergit what I said 'bout the game on this place!"

We had barely pulled onto the Pass Creek Road when the sheriff's office called on the radio to report that the neighboring ranch foreman needed to talk with me right away. Doesn't news travel fast? I told Mel that the culprits probably wanted to "confess their sins" and we hurried on east towards the ranch. Boy, was I ever dreaming!

Shortly, we pulled up in front of the ranch office. A freshly washed four-wheel-drive pickup with matching stock trailer stood amidst dirty vehicles in the ranch's parking area. It was apparent that the boys had been busy little beavers since noon, covering their tracks. Mel stayed with our pickup to guard the evidence. Several ranchhands were lounging about when I entered the office building. I recognized two of the hands who were the most likely to have been involved with the poaching, one of whom was the foreman's son. They nervously exited into an adjacent room, leaving the door ajar.

Swaggering up to me, the foreman blurted out, in his nauseating drawl, "Button, ya-all had bedda back off this hea elk deal with ma neighba'. Ya ain't gonna win it!" The nervy s.o.b. had made a request, through the sheriff's office, asking me to stop by so he could intimidate me! I knew the guy had balls, hanging out of his ears! Both he and his son had the full line of obnox-ious traits provided by genes from that well-known obtrusive and overbear-ing race of Texan all too often found up North. I asked the arrogant cow boss if he had requested that I stop by only to threaten me, or if he had some-thing constructive to add to the case. He assured me that he had "meant it only as good advice – for yer own good" and that he had nothing else to add. It was quite obvious that I wasn't going to receive any confessions here.

The Texans had probably shot all three elk. They may have felt somewhat responsible – at least enough to try intimidation – for their neighbor's dilem-ma. They weren't, though, quite willing to face prosecution to protect him.

He wasn't *that* good of a neighbor. And hadn't they shared their ill-gotten meat with him? I left the brief confab both frustrated and disgusted, but no less determined.

Mel and I had probably stumbled onto a rather traditional neighborhood elk shoot that usually went off much better. It was doubtful now that the other two elk would be found even if a search warrant could be obtained.

As the sun was setting, we left for town. I had received enough advice that afternoon to last for a while. Tomorrow would be another day.

The next morning I went to the elk kill sites to take photos and to continue the investigation. I spent quite a while reading what sign remained in the melting snow. Chinook winds had started blowing during the night, and the tracks had become distorted. It was obvious that the poachers had entered and left from the same location on the county road. The snowplow, however, had obliterated all sign on the road, severing the trail that otherwise would have tied the Texans to the crime scene.

The scenario seemed obvious. The elk herd had been spotted either the evening before, or on the morning of the hunt. The three elk were killed at daybreak. The poachers had approached the herd from the county road to the east and downwind of the animals. Then, each ranch got a portion of the ill-gotten harvest.

In my mind's eye, I reviewed what we could prove. We had caught the old rancher with the elk "red-handed." The illegal possession charge could be proved without doubt. And it would be obvious to a jury that he had received fruits of a crime. The evidence at the scene indicated that the Texans had helped load the rancher's elk on his hay sled. From the air we had missed the Texans by no more than 15 minutes. Both time and circumstance now favored them. Now, unless someone came forth with testimony, they were going to luck out!

The county attorney cringed when he saw the defendant's name on the citation. We discussed the case at great length. The attorney felt that since all the actors involved wished to play hardball the old-timer would have to stand in court alone. He said that a fair jury would have to convict the prominent rancher on the illegal possession charge. Of course, certain influential sentiments could still favor the old pioneer. But we didn't realize to what extent this would be true.

We soon learned that the defendant's nephew, a Sheridan attorney, would represent his uncle, and that they had requested a jury trial. Because the criminal charge was a misdemeanor, a petit (six-person) jury, would hear the case. The county sheriff would select the potential jurors. And he could select them just about any way that he wished to. He could pick names at random from a phone book or he could select candidates off the street. As long as the potential jurors were still warm and voted in the county they could serve. Since prosecution and defense each had three preemptory challenges, 12 prospective jurors would be impaneled.

After several postponements, the big day finally arrived. At the start of the jury selection the jury box was chock-full of rancher-types. All twelve of them. Judge Garbutt had to tell several of the stockmen to remove their hats in the courtroom. He told them that it wasn't necessary, however, to take off their neckerchiefs. The high sheriff had chosen to pick all the prospective jurors at the Sheridan Elks Lodge, a favorite wintertime hangout for area ranchers. The sheriff had dealt our cards off the bottom of the deck. The prosecution had been had! Now it took absolutely no imagination to predict the outcome. It would be an exercise in futility.

We went along with the game and struck three ranchers from the list. And the defense struck three ranchers from the list. Then, guess what? That left six "impartial" ranchers to serve! The jury was definitely comprised of the defendant's "peers." Just how "tried and true" they were, remained to be seen. But not for long.

The prosecution proved beyond a doubt that the defendant had an illegal elk in his possession. Circumstantial evidence showed that the defendant had been the recipient of the ill-gotten goods. A fair jury must find the defendant guilty.

The defense put the old rancher on the stand to testify. He simply told of salvaging a dead elk that he had found on his land.

That jury deliberated an entire five minutes. And of course the verdict was "Not Guilty!"

After court was adjourned, a group of stockmen were overheard agreeing that the verdict should demonstrate to the public that it's all right for ranchers to kill game whenever they please. Their rationale seemed to be, "Everything on my land is mine and everything on your land (leased public land) is also mine!"

For a while that morning I thought I had been somehow caught up in a time-warp, and that it was actually the 1860s, rather than the 1960s. This court experience would serve as an excellent reminder to me through the years. In law enforcement, as in life in general, you had better always figure in the "human factor."

The Pass Creek cowboys held a great victory gloat that evening.

Oh, by the way, the sheriff was the defendant's brother-in-law!

Bullheaded

The vast western grasslands were free for the grazing, and beginning in the 1860s, stockgrowers took advantage of the situation.

By the turn of the century, the overgrazed western ranges were in a deplorable condition. Eventually, both state and federal agencies were created to steward public land use. Some folks expected to see improvement on the previously abused public rangeland now that experts would be in charge of it. This was not to be. The stockman had been king since the settlement of the West, and he still swung a lot of meat.

The only effective way to improve any overgrazed range is to reduce the amount of livestock using it. This sounds rather simple to accomplish, but it wasn't. Any reduction of livestock on these lands would come only after a bloody fight. And the powerful land barons would take the fight to Congress if necessary.

Forest rangers who tried cutting livestock numbers to improve the ranges were soon history. Politics was always brought to bear whenever and wherever good land stewardship was preached. Restoration of the rangelands seemed to be an impossible feat. The western prairies had never really recovered from a century of abuse. What were the guardians of our public lands to do?

Federal soil scientists came up with a plan they said would solve the overgrazing problem and at the same time was sure to be palatable to grazing permittees. Now there would be no need to bloody themselves by suggesting livestock population reduction on public lands.

Many years of land abuse by overgrazing had caused the retrogression of plant species from climax to a poorer condition with much less grass available to the livestock. The soil scientists would simply increase the amount of grass by eradicating the forbs and sagebrush. The elated range experts told the ranchers that they could even expect increased grazing use as soon as grasses replaced the weeds and forbs. Eradication of the sagebrush would be the answer to all overgrazing problems. Why wouldn't ranchers support such a program?

Wild Journey

Wyoming game wardens on backcountry patrol in the Big Horn Mountains. Photo: Dave Bragonier

In the early 1950s the U.S. Agriculture Stabilization and Conservation Service, U.S. Forest Service, Bureau of Land Management, state land agencies and ranchers teamed up to begin an all-out sagebrush eradication effort in an attempt to restore the western grasslands.

Sagebrush eradication began in Wyoming in 1952. By 1964, 505,000 acres of sagebrush had been treated in Wyoming, mostly with the financial aid of the taxpayers through the cooperating ASCS. The technique generally used was the application of the herbicide 2,4-D by aerial spraying. Many thousands of Forest Service and BLM acres were sprayed by the ranch operators with the blessings of those federal agencies.

Wyoming's big game herds had staged a comeback from their lowest levels in history, caused by the settling of the West. Starting in the late 1800s, market-hunters and settlers had almost wiped out the larger species of game animals by the first part of this century.

The first major step towards restoring wildlife was taken in 1899 when the Wyoming legislature gave enforcement powers to the game laws already on the books. By World War II, big game herds frequented most areas of the state. Hunting pressure was cut dramatically during the five-year war period because many of the state's hunters were overseas fighting. Because there were several years of reduced harvest, the herds continued to flourish. The increase of forbs and sagebrush on the ranges favored the browsing species, particularly mule deer and antelope. By the time the great sagebrush eradication scheme had begun, Wyoming's big game herds were restored and doing very well.

During this era, wildlife had few acknowledged friends in federal and state government outside the game department. This ambivalence carried through to the University of Wyoming. Game and fish department personnel dreaded the annual game season setting meetings with the federal agencies and the stockgrowers' associations. The game department was constantly pressured to reduce the big game herds even though seldom is there competition between wild browsers and domestic grazers under normal open range conditions. All the overgrazed ranges in the state were blamed on the wildlife. Game management in those days was not much fun. Always, the hue and cry was that too much game had taken too much forage away from too few cows and sheep. Add to this the University of Wyoming's animal scientists who were constantly lurking in the shadows to slash out at the department's hamstrings at every opportunity.

The division of agriculture economics of the university published a circular, *A Survey of Big Sagebrush Control in Wyoming*, which touted all the wonderful reasons for sagebrush eradication. Printed in November of 1965, the survey lightly brushed away any concern for wildlife using the area, and concentrated on the possibilities of increasing livestock use on the treated rangeland by a hundred percent or more. It is noteworthy to relate the very unscientific method the university came up with to determine what effect the spray project might have on wildlife. They simply asked the ranchers what they thought! University scientists quoting the ranchers concluded: "No discernible change in use by the game species but there were some reports of increased use of sprayed areas... Use of sprayed areas by sage grouse increased slightly in all four seasons."

Ranchers certainly have a feel for how game animals are doing in their areas. But, like the rest of us, they are only human. The trouble with the poll was only the landowners who stood to benefit from the project were queried. This likely produced a bias for sagebrush eradication.

The university release mentions only one disadvantage connected with sagebrush eradication: "The difficulty in obtaining sufficient capital to eradicate as much sagebrush as desired." Some of the ranchers polled by the professors desired a means of elimination of the "dead sagebrush stalks." Still other ranchers felt that, "The stalks definitely benefited the range by collecting snow in drifts and preventing it from blowing off." Another profound conclusion was offered: "Dead sage also provides some shelter for newborn or young lambs and calves as well as shelter and concealment for sage grouse and game animals."

Healthy, untreated, sagebrush does a better job of both sheltering new-borns and holding snow!

The university publication goes on to use the low war-years harvest before the sagebrush eradication to compare with the much higher harvests of the early 60's, implying a dramatic increase in wildlife because of the sagebrush

Sagebrush bench on Dry Fork of the Little Horn River prior to eradication program. Photo: Dave Bragonier

eradication program. The university scientists really grasp at straws when the publication continues, "It has generally been thought that sagebrush-type range is important as deer and elk winter range and as sites for these animals to give birth. Some question exists, however, as to the actual value of sage-brush for winter forage. Although appreciable quantities of sagebrush are ingested by livestock and game, especially deer, (Julius) Nasy found that essential-oil content of sagebrush is high. It might adversely affect digestibil-ity, not only of sagebrush but of other ingested feeds, because of the action of these essential oils on rumen micro-organisms."

The quoted paper was Julius Nasy's "Effects of Essential Oils of Sagebrush on Deer Rumen Microbial Function," published in the *Journal of Wildlife Management,* in October 1964. What should be concluded from this paper? That it's a mystery why deer have survived in the West for thousands of years? It seems quite obvious the study proved only what its authors wanted

Elk calf resting among sagebrush on a bench above Dry Fork of the Little Horn Canyon. Photo: Dave Bragonier

to prove. But surely there's no such thing as a biased scientist!

Really, scientists are a lot like attorneys. They both can always create some kind of case – no matter how feeble – for the other side. It would seem that sagebrush and deer have co-existed rather well for eons. One more quotation from this University of Wyoming publication is worthy of mention to demonstrate the sheer prejudice involved. It expounds, "Because sagebrush in Wyoming is prevalent, elk and also deer may be forced to accept such sites for giving birth, whether or not they prefer them."

Wildlife biologist Calvin King served the Wyoming Game and Fish Department for 40 years. In his book, *History of Wildlife in the Big Horn Basin of Wyoming,* the respected biologist says, "The game tagging operations that I have been involved in clearly portray the importance of sagebrush to calving and fawning activities. The sagebrush adjacent to timbered areas is of vital importance to elk calving activities. Sagebrush depressions and drainages particularly those on the south, west and east slopes are desirable elk calving and deer fawning sites." Cal spent most of his career working with wildlife on the west slope of the Big Horn Mountains.

The sagebrush benches of the Dry Fork of the Little Horn River drainage are important big game birthing grounds that lie adjacent to the Kerns Elk Pasture on the north end of the Big Horn Mountains. Each spring at the peak of the elk calving season, which is about the first week in June in Wyoming, I would ride the sagebrush and grassland meadows scattered for approximately eight miles up and down the shelf above the creek. With my horses I would discreetly camp at Double Springs and spend several days, quietly observing the event and taking a trend count of the elk using the grounds. I did this each of the six springs, from 1963 through 1968.

Sometimes Norbert Faass, a neighboring warden, would accompany me on these trips. Norb and I enjoyed working in the hills together, and I learned a great deal about wildlife from him.

Unlike the upper reaches of the Dry Fork drainage, the pristine sagebrush benches below the Kerns Cow Camp had remained untouched by herbicides. The Dry Fork's headwater, accessed by a two-track road from Burgess Junction, was one of the first sagebrush eradication projects (1952) in the state. By the 1960s, few old sage brush "stalks" remained in the spray-site. Although scattered sprigs of new sage growth were evident in the area, no cover was available for wildlife larger than small rodents. Old game and fish records dating back to the 1940s show that game wardens had tagged many elk calves on this location before the eradication of the sagebrush.

During my six years of elk calving grounds census work on the Dry Fork, the average count was 146 elk, mostly cows with their calves, below Kerns Cow Camp. A number of mule deer also used the area for birthing. During those years, very few elk and deer were observed in or near the old eradicated area above the cow camp even though the sprayers had left untreated a narrow strip of sagebrush on the fringe of the meadow. In fact, I was never able to document the presence of a single cow elk with a newborn calf in proximity to the old spray-site. This would indicate that a much larger expanse of this "fringe" cover is necessary to be of any value to big game animals for birthing sites.

Sagebrush is the ideal birthing cover for elk and mule deer because the mother can conceal her young, yet keep an eye out for predators. Sagebrush offers both sunshine and shade to the newborn, whichever is preferred at the moment. When the only available birthing cover is the cold and dark conifer timber, newborn survival rate will no doubt go down. Sagebrush is the birthing cover preferred by most of Wyoming's big game animals. The sagebrush/grassland communities, both in the mountains and in the basins, are very important habitats for western wildlife.

During tough winter weather, when the snows cover all other vegetation, sagebrush becomes the main ingredient for survival of many wild animals, offering them both food and shelter. High in protein, sagebrush has also saved a myriad of livestock over the years.

In his book, biologist King comments on sagebrush eradication: "Spray treatment of sagebrush communities prior to the time guidelines were formulated (1975) resulted in significant losses of deer habitat. A prime example is the headwaters of North and South Paintrock (Creeks) on the Bighorn Forest. Prior to treatment, the area had a good deer population. After treatment, the deer population decreased.

King continues, "Another example where deer populations decreased after extensive sagebrush treatment is illustrated in the Prospect Creek drainage. The area was prime deer winter range habitat in the 1950s and 1960s."

And then it finally happened! Bighorn National Forest officials said they intended to spray the sagebrush meadows below Kerns Cow Camp on the Dry Fork of the Little Horn drainage to enhance grazing opportunities![1] I objected vehemently to this proposal because it would continue the destruction of the area's big game birthing grounds.

In the rangelands, most champions of wildlife within forest service and BLM ranks had yet to emerge from their closets. Those who ventured out risked a swift transfer. Robert Ridings' Bighorn Forest was especially notorious for using this method of discipline for any such plucky outburst from an employee.

Sagebrush eradication and other projects to increase livestock grazing on public lands were common at the time. Federal officials called such programs "Wildlife/Livestock Enhancement Projects." The word "wildlife" was included as a ploy to gain the support of sportsmen. It was a rare occasion when wildlife gained more than it lost from such projects.

During the 1967 elk calving season, I took the assistant forest supervisor, the ranger, and a range biologist on my annual trend count in the area. We observed 137 elk and several dozen mule deer using the yet untreated area, and only five elk (without calves) in a two-mile stretch in the proximity of the old sprayed area. At the time, the officials seemed to demonstrate genuine concern for the elk. But after they returned to their offices their true colors also returned. Forest Service officials told the public that they would proceed with their lower Dry Fork sagebrush eradication proposal.

I was vocal in my opposition to the project. In Wyoming, game wardens share game management responsibilities with the area biologist, at least that's the plan. Initially, both the biologist and the district supervisor also voiced their opposition to the sagebrush eradication project. But as the issue became more heated and political, their voices faded to complete silence. The Sheridan County Sportsmen's Club and others, however, remained united in opposition to the project. Sadly, the day of the wildlife advocate coalitions had yet to arrive.

In an attempt to gain sportsman support for the project, the Bighorn

---

[1] The major livestock grazing permitee to benefit from the "enhanced grazing" was not your struggling fourth-generation ranching family, but a wealthy, non-resident, hobby rancher.

National Forest officials again began to expound on how the project would greatly enhance the forage for both livestock and big game animals. The officials also claimed that the overgrazed range was due, in part, to elk use. These were timeworn ploys used by the Feds whenever there's a livestock overgrazing problem. The truth to this could easily be found by visiting one of the Forest Service's own range study-plots after the livestock grazing season in the fall of the year. These plots were erected (before the elk debate) to demonstrate livestock range use. The enclosures were constructed of the regular, low, sheep-cattle tight material to keep out only livestock (their sole concern at the time of construction). A deer or an elk can jump in and out of the enclosures with ease. After the livestock had left the range completely devoid of grass in the fall, the thick vegetation within the plot remained untouched.

Within a few months I received notice of my transfer from the Dayton warden district. I asked the chief warden the reason for the move. He informed me that the area's new game and fish commission member, a rancher appointed by the governor to serve a four-year term, had requested my transfer because I was going against the wishes of both forest service officials and the stockmen in my opposition to the sagebrush spray project. "And furthermore," the commission member told the chief warden, "Dave is being very *bullheaded* in his opposition. The other involved department personnel knew when to back off!" Transferring me was, politically, the easy way out for the department.

The next evening I drove over to Wolf and confronted the new commission member regarding his request for my transfer. He immediately told me that he was very unhappy about my opposition to the Dry Fork sagebrush spray proposal. "And besides that," he said, "a coupla' years ago, you arrested my hired man just for buyin' a resident hunting license – and you fined him! Maybe he hadn't lived in the state long enough – but he intended to live here – and he didn't make enough money to buy a non-resident license, and I thought at the time that it was a damned chicken shit deal!" "And then another time," he continued, "you pinched my neighbor – just for shootin' a damned grouse! Hell, even though the season was closed – it was on his own place! You just don't seem ta know how ta get along with folks!"

I got in trouble for doing exactly what I was paid to do: catching poachers and attempting to protect game habitat. Such are the woes of the politically appointed commission form of government.

Anyway, I was transferred, and wildlife lost more habitat.

Today, the federal land agencies include wildlife in their multiple use agendas.

Wild Journey

Most authorities now recognize the importance of sagebrush to western wildlife and the watersheds.

The Dry Fork of the Little Horn River is again under siege. This time, the area's wildlife is threatened by those who would construct a hydrolectric dam within the pristine canyon.

The Cody Country

The Long Season

The Cody Country has long been a favorite hunting ground for mankind. Native Americans stalked game in the Absaroka Mountains centuries before John Colter and other mountain men came along. Later still, William F. "Buffalo Bill" Cody arrived there and built a hunting lodge and a town along the banks of the Shoshone River.

The region has three federally designated wilderness areas – the North Absaroka, Washakie and Teton that join Yellowstone Park to make up one of the largest remaining expanses of contiguous wilderness in North America south of Canada.

The locality's diverse wildlife includes elk, moose, mule deer, whitetail deer, bighorn sheep, mountain goat, pronghorn antelope, both black bear and grizzly and mountain lion. The area also has many trout-filled streams and lakes. Because of this wealth of wildlife, a multitude of folks take advantage of the resource – some for pleasure and others for profit – but not all of them play by the rules.

I transferred to the area in the early 1970s.

Before my actual move there, I attended a public hearing on hunting seasons held by game department managers, at Cody, and received my indoctrination on how the local game merchants manipulated the process.

Having nothing better to do the next day, I drove up the North Fork of the Shoshone River highway to Yellowstone Park's East Gate, just sort of looking over a portion of my new district. On the casual drive up the river I discovered the carcasses of a moose, an elk and two mule deer at different locations near the highway. All the animals had been shot and nothing had been removed from the carcasses. And they had not first been crippled by a collision with a vehicle. It was apparent that someone was shooting game animals from the road just for whatever thrill they might receive from doing so. This was a preview of what was to come.

As the moving van was pulling away from the Cody warden station I began hearing from the neighbors about the area's year-round poaching problem.

One persistent rumor that summer had a Wapiti resident shooting a bighorn ram from his porch early that spring. The proud poacher had supposedly displayed his illegal trophy to various friends and neighbors. Then, his wife smuggled the ram's head, inside a garbage can, to an illicit taxidermist he knew back in his hometown of Chicago. A number of witnesses were found who were willing to testify against the violator even though he warned them he had Mafia connections. In this case, *corpus delicti* (body of the crime) was established based on the testimony of several witnesses, and the great white hunter was convicted.

Cody area big game seasons are as liberal as any place on Earth, with hunts from September through December. Even so, it was common knowledge that many hunters waited for the "long season," after the legal hunting season is closed, to kill elk and deer when the animals arrive on their winter ranges at the time when they are most vulnerable.

Long season hunters usually do their thing late at night with the aid of a spotlight. Here, they would work the North Fork of the Shoshone River if after an elk, and the South Fork of that river when they wanted to kill a deer.

A number of North Fork lodge owners and South Fork ranchers asked if I would become irritated, as had the former warden, if I received calls in the middle of the night reporting gunshots. I thanked them for their interest and requested that they give me a chance.

Although the use of artificial light to aid in the hunting of game animals has never been allowed by Wyoming statute, the lack of such a law governing the hunting of predators (coyote, fox, raccoon, skunk, jackrabbit, etc.) made it extremely difficult to apprehend nighttime poachers. And poachers really loved it. If a game warden checked violators who were spotlighting before they had killed a game animal, the poachers were, of course, predator hunting. The minute a poacher scored on a game animal, the spotlight was immediately turned off and he was homeward bound with his ill-gotten goods.[1]

Many ranchers and other citizens would report all spotlighting activity they observed, and most winter nights, especially on weekends, Wyoming's game wardens were kept busy receiving and checking out the calls. On one very cold and nasty January night, separate parties poached five deer at Cody area locations between 10:00 p.m. and 4:00 a.m. Only one poacher was apprehended.

---

[1] The state of Wyoming now has an adequate law governing the taking of predators with aid of artificial light.

During the early part of this wild and sleepless era, I was the only game warden available in the Cody area. The illegal hunting activity had me running ragged. Lovell game warden Gary Shorma and Greybull warden Terry Cleveland would often spell me by taking late-night patrols. The two wardens caught an individual with an elk within two hours after I had completed a patrol. The poacher later admitted to checking out my garage before going hunting that night.

At the beginning of this trying period, neither of the two Park County justices of the peace in Cody believed in jail sentences for game law violators although the law provided for up to six-month sentences. And although the law allowed a judge to revoke hunting and fishing privileges, they also hesitated to take these privileges away. The $200 fines the judges were meting out had little to no effect on the poaching activity. Such light penalties for poaching brought only chuckles from the poaching element, and the illegal activities continued. In fact, during a seven-week period beginning in December, 14 elk and deer poachers were apprehended for taking big game animals out of season.

One deer poacher was an ex-con with a drug addiction. During the execution of a search warrant on his South Fork cabin, we discovered several pipe-bombs on the kitchen table. He was sent back to the federal hotel for a couple more years. The bomber told another inmate of his plan to "waste" me when he got out of the big house. He was going to place "reflector-tape" on my department pickup so he would recognize my outfit when he met it at night. Such an "elaborate" scheme couldn't fail!

At long last both judges admitted that fines alone were not curbing the problem. Once the judges began imposing jail sentences and revoking violators' hunting privileges things quieted down. Illegal hunting, however, is never completely stopped. There are too many poaching hot-spots and too few game wardens to cover them. Cody sportsmen and other good citizens were ready for a change. A number of them offered to help in any way they legally could.

With the help of Park County sheriff Harley Kinkade and his undersheriff Bill Brewer, a citizens' patrol was organized. The members acted only as eyes and ears for law enforcement. Each patrol always included two members in possession of a police-band radio, and the teams were required to check with law enforcement dispatch when going both on and off patrol. All crimes observed, not just game violations, were immediately reported. Members provided their own vehicles, and fuel was donated.

Formation of the citizens' patrol was published, and frequent reminders of its existence were advertised. Law violators now had to watch for more than just law enforcement vehicles. It worked. Citizen patrols combined with strict law enforcement further slowed poaching activity.

In this age of government assistance programs and community kitchens, there's no longer an excuse for subsistence poaching. Today's poachers rarely take proper care of game meat, unless it is to be sold. That tells the story: Killing for the family table is seldom a poacher's first thought. Poachers poach either for profit or just for the pure hell of it!

At one time I kept a list of welfare recipients to whom I would give confiscated and road-salvaged game. I have heard many thankless comments such as:

> "We don't want any trout. Fish poison both me and my wife."
> "We already get more free meat than we can use. Give it to some one who really needs it!"
> "Will you also cut the deer up and package it for me?"

Instead, I sought out those proud and hard-working folks who would rather starve than go on the public dole.

The Black Marketeers

During the latter part of the 19th century and the early part of the 20th, market hunting was mostly for game meat, and some for the plumage of certain bird species. This exploitation of wildlife for monetary gain brought several large wild animals and numerous species of wild fowl dangerously close to extinction, prompting legislative action on both state and federal levels to stop the wanton slaughter. Laws designed to protect and manage wildlife were soon passed in most states and in Congress.

Now, other market-hunting activities threaten our wildlife. This time it is not the sale of game meat, but for the sale of other wild animal parts. It's no longer the poaching of flamingos and egrets for their plumage, but the illicit trade in raptor feathers and talons. Today's wildlife black market also includes the high-dollar sale of illegal hunts for game animals.

For the purpose of this discussion, a black marketeer is anyone who profits from an illegal pursuit dealing in wildlife.

Poaching for profit today is widespread and targets numerous species of wildlife for different reasons and for unrelated markets. The only similarity is the huge monetary profit this illicit trafficking produces. Because Wyoming has no law prohibiting the sale of legally taken antlers, horns, hides or heads, the enforcement of black market wildlife trafficking is at times compromised.

Take for instance the trafficking in antlers from the deer family for the Oriental-Asian aphrodisiac and medicinal market. The Asian population in this country and abroad believe "ungdam" (Korean for bear gallbladder), and "nogyong" (Korean for antler) can cure a wide variety of ills. Their belief stems from a centuries-old culture. The "ungdam" and "nogyong" are processed into a powder which the Asians take internally. Modern science has found no medicinal value in either antlers or gallbladders.

Antlers are collected in several different ways, depending on the conscience of those involved in the market. A number of antlers are collected from winter ranges of deer and elk where the animals shed them annually. The multitude of individuals searching for these antlers while the herds are still on their winter range stresses the animals at a time when their tolerance level is at a minimum. The shed antler can readily be identified as such, if not tampered with, by examination of the burr end of the antler where it attached to the skull. With the exception of the National Elk Refuge at Jackson, and the national parks and monuments, it is not illegal to collect antlers in national forests and other places in Wyoming. However, such activity may be restricted to a time after wintering wildlife have left an area.

Antlers with the skull cap attached have obviously come from a dead animal. But are the antlers from a legal kill, winter kill, or a poached or other illegally obtained source, (such as a stolen trophy head)? In recent years, dealers have been paying up to $10 a pound for brown (fresh) antlers, and somewhat less for white (old) antlers, with no questions asked. The two antlers from a prime bull elk may weigh up to 20 pounds apiece.

Thieves have stolen the antlers from the yards, archways and outside walls of many western mountain lodges, ranches and homes. Now, robbers are burglarizing buildings and stealing antlers off inside walls. When this lucrative market first began in North America a few years back, antler theft was a major crime in several western counties.

Blood or velvet antlers, those still forming on a living animal, are worth much more than the others and dealers in the field pay several times more per pound for them. Asians will pay more than $100 an ounce for the processed article. Since blood antlers are prime for the market for a short period in the spring and early summer, there is small chance for any legally taken wild antlers to enter the market.

A number of commercial game farms are now raising members of the deer family specifically for the lucrative blood antler market. Investigation of any suspect wild blood antlers in this market becomes very difficult once dealers have cut up and mixed both wild and game farm antlers together into one lot.

Bear (black or grizzly) gallbladders are in demand for generally the same purpose as the antlers by the same ethnic group. Bear paws are also considered very much of a table delicacy by Orientals, and they will pay ridiculous prices for them.

A California case involving many man-days of undercover work by that state's game enforcement officers and lasting several months brought to light some very disturbing facts. Officers found that as many as 100 individual houndsmen were hunting bears with their dogs both during and out of that state's legal bear season, mainly to obtain only the gallbladders and paws from the bears. Seizure of the parts of 55 bears by the department was involved in just this one operation. One can only guess at the total number of bears killed during recent years by this type of activity.

There is some trafficking of Wyoming bear parts. It is reported that the supply is not meeting the present demand. If half of the world's population is Asian, and with an ever-increasing Asian population in the United States, we definitely have a problem.

Trade in illegally taken raptors (any bird of prey) and raptor parts is also a multimillion-dollar business. This market is thriving because collectors are buying Native American arts and crafts items made from the feathers. An Indian war bonnet made with eagle feathers can bring $5,000 dollars. One tail feather from a golden eagle will bring a minimum of $50. Whole carcasses of golden or bald eagles can bring $500 each, according to the U. S. Fish and Wildlife Service.

Another serious illicit wildlife business is the marketing of big game hunts to wealthy clientele. Such large-dollar "bogus license" hunts are now being carried out by big game outfitters throughout the inter-mountain West. This illegal market is kept alive and well by a huge reservoir of moneyed slob hunters who hunt big game animals either with or without proper licenses. These unlawful hunts usually, but not always, take place at a time during legal hunting seasons when such operations are more easily disguised. The outfitter will often pay a guide, a friend or the camp cook for the use of their license-tag which will be placed on a client's illegal kill. Oftentimes, those involved in such hunts don't even worry themselves about such "small matters" as hunting licenses. Either way it's the same: Honest citizens are being cheated out of their wildlife.

In Wyoming, the State Board of Outfitters and Professional Guides is the licensing authority for that business. The public often hears much to-do about how "coyote" (unlicensed) outfitters are taking business away from "honest" licensed outfitters. Even so, licensed outfitters still manage to book their fair share of unlicensed slob hunters.

Such cases can be very complex and quite difficult to piece together for a successful prosecution. Quite often an investigation of this kind will be ongoing for several years. Usually there are a number of potential witnesses, but many of them were most likely involved in the illegal activity. The rare guide, wrangler or cook who may not have been directly implicated will still be reluctant to give testimony because of the real possibility of being black-balled from the business if they assist law officers in any way. Still, a number of these cases have been successfully prosecuted.

A Cody area outfitter and several of his wealthy clients were convicted of obtaining and using fraudulent elk hunting licenses. To ensure clients' chances in the nonresident limited-quota elk license draw, they would

Wild Journey

Outfitter clients' illegal trophies. Photo: Fred Herbel. Wyoming Game and Fish Department.

submit multiple license applications. Each client would submit one application using his proper name and several more under aliases with similar physical descriptions. When a client would draw more than one license, a friend would accompany the group on the hunt and use the bogus license, or the client himself would take two hunts and kill two or more elk that year.

During 1995, four western Wyoming outfitters, four guides and 51 clients were convicted on state and federal charges of hunting license abuse. These clients were found guilty and paid more than $140,000 in fines and restitution. The outfitters were given hefty fines and one of them, along with his guide, were sentenced to four months in federal prison.[1]

More recently, Wyoming game and fish enforcement specialist Jim Oudin, with the assistance of federal wardens, put the quietus to another Cody country illegal big game hunting operation. This outfitter served one

---

[1] The federal "Lacey Act" prohibits the importation or transportation across state lines of illegal wildlife. Another federal law prohibits conspiracy to commit an interstate wildlife crime. Agents of the United States Fish and Wildlife Service enforce federal wildlife laws.

year in a federal prison for his felony convictions of conspiring with and outfitting several dozen improperly licensed non-resident hunters in violation of federal laws. The outfitter's clients transported many of their illegal animals across state lines. The outfitter could have also received up to $750,000 and a prison term of 15 years for the three felony counts with which he was charged. Five of his clients together paid $30,000 in fines. Many struck deals with the prosecution and received reduced sentences in exchange for their testimony against the outfitter.

The convicted outfitter told a news reporter, "I'm not proud of what happened here, but it's undoubtedly part of the hunting business around here. This has been going on for over 15 years in every outfit I've worked for!"

Confiscated elk heads were scheduled to become black market trophies. Photo: Wyoming Game and Fish Department

The outfitter board allowed the toppled outfitter's wife to take over the operation.

Outfitters caught with their pants down in the middle of such schemes often attempt to justify their illegal actions by saying they can't survive within the law because not enough of their clients draw hunting licenses each year. While it's sink or swim in any other business, outfitters are demanding that lawmakers allot each of them – good hands and sorry alike – a guaranteed number of non-resident big game hunting licenses each year to dole out as they please. Outfitters say if they were assured a fixed number of licenses they would need not be bad boys.

These professional hunters can be categorized in the same way as regular hunters: there are too few within their ranks who are true sportsmen. The fact that only a mere handful of their numbers, and always the same handful, ever reports game law violations to authorities pretty much tells their sad story!

Outfitters and guides do provide a necessary service to an important segment of the hunting community. A few of them do an excellent job and have high ethical standards. But there are too many chronic offenders among their ranks who are involved in various illegal wildlife schemes for big bucks. And those high-rolling headhunters are certainly out there. A letter sent by an outfitter to a prospective client regarding an illegal sheep hunt was seized by federal officers. The outfitter guaranteed a record-book ram, and if the sheep scored over 200 points, the price would be $20,000. Hunters wishing to possess a legitimate Rocky Mountain bighorn sheep license pay from $20,000 to $50,000 for one at legal auctions held in Wyoming and Montana. The second place world record mule deer head is said to have recently sold for $50,000.

Hard-core poaching for profit and/or personal gain is targeting trophy-sized big game animals. These thugs, usually posing as photographers, are now striking big game winter ranges throughout the West at an alarming rate. Just average-sized trophy mule deer and elk heads may bring over $4000 each, and bighorn sheep heads in that category can bring upwards of $12,000. Of course world-class heads will bring considerably more dough. While the black market is presently going great-guns in large buck mule deer heads, the trafficking in trophy heads of all the large game species also remains very healthy. After killing the finest specimen they can find, these bandits swiftly retreat with only the heads, leaving the meat behind to rot. After just a few minutes, the poachers have fled the scene. Because the entire process doesn't take long, it makes the arrest of poachers all the more difficult.

A number of years ago, an unscrupulous outfitter was booking slob hunters in Texas. He would guarantee prospective clients a minimum three-quarter-curl ram at a time when there would be no competition from other hunters. This black marketeer was taking "out of season" bighorn sheep hunts in the Cody area during late winter and early spring. He would take his clients hunting on the animals' winter ranges where the slob hunters

Horns and capes taken from poached pronghorn antelope. Photo: Dave Bragonier.

could shoot a trophy ram either out a vehicle window or after a short walk. By taking advantage of the wild sheep in this manner the outfitter had a thriving business, that is until he booked a United States Fish and Wildlife Service agent. This outfitter was fined less than what one of his illegal hunts would cost a client.

About the same time, a northwest Wyoming poaching ring was also working over the bighorns' winter ranges. Word had it that at one time the ring had nearly 20 bighorn ram heads for distribution on the black market. This gang would switch to poaching trophy-sized pronghorn antelope for the California market sometime before the legal hunt on that species would begin. One fall, a search warrant was served just minutes before seven caped-out antelope heads were to leave for the West Coast. While several of the hoodlums were convicted for the offenses, this law enforcement effort barely slowed the gang down.

All this repulsive activity amounts to much more than theft of wildlife from honest citizens and legitimate hunters. It is also threatening the overall welfare of the herds.

Game managers know the importance of maintaining sufficient numbers of the largest and most intelligent of the male segment to sustain the genetic health of a herd. When setting hunting seasons, good managers will attempt to guard against too heavy a harvest from this important male segment. And over-harvest of these clever old patriarchs during fair chase situations seldom occurs. However, it's an entirely different story after the animals move onto their winter ranges, lose much of their wariness and are most vulnerable to poachers.

The legislatures of many states, including Wyoming,[2] have now enacted laws to address this problem. A number of these winter range poachers have been apprehended for killing big game animals just for their heads, and charged under the new laws. Many of them have received heavy fines, suspended sentences and lengthy hunting privilege suspensions. But a $10,000 fine is nothing to someone in that kind of business, and hunting privilege suspensions mean little to a poacher. Judges must begin giving these derelicts lengthy jail sentences and legislatures must provide for confiscation of all equipment, including vehicles, used in the commission of a serious poaching act.

Trophy-hunting miscreants, desiring easy prey, are also desecrating our national treasures by killing unwary game animals accustomed only to photographers and sightseers.

In September of 1993, a brazen Salt Lake City poacher shot and killed a seven-by-eight point bull elk near a major roadway in Yellowstone National Park. He took only the animal's massive antlers. Before the magnificent specimen was killed, the bull had been enjoyed by thousands of tourists and photographers. The thief was apprehended when a taxidermist recognized the antlers from a photograph of the animal in a magazine article relating the death of the bull elk.

More recently, a months-long undercover operation helped wildlife agents catch several hunters, along with their outfitter-guide, for poaching elk and deer inside Dinosaur National Monument on the Utah-Colorado border. The hunters received penalties ranging from stiff fines to a prison term to revocation for life of hunting privileges in Colorado, Utah and six other Western states. Eight men, including a prominent Wichita, Kansas plastic surgeon and a Dallas, Texas millionaire, were indicted in 1998 as a result of "Operation Dinosaur," an investigation into unlawful big game hunts in the

---

[2] Wyoming's so-called "winter range law," enacted in 1993, is designed in part to combat winter range poaching. A person who is convicted of knowingly taking an antlered or horned big game animal, lion or bear out of season or without the proper license faces a penalty of between $5,000 and $10,000 to which may be added up to one year in jail. State law does not provide, however, for the confiscation of a convicted poacher's equipment.

national monument. A Steamboat Springs, Colorado outfitter would take wealthy clients inside the park, charging between $4,000 and $10,000 for each illegal hunt. The outfitter was sentenced to one year and one day in prison, three years supervised release and was given a $10,000 fine.

This ugly problem exists because society has produced perverted individuals who are so obsessed with large big game heads that they are determined to possess them, no matter what. Many of these deviates pursue their obsession both during and after legal seasons. Wildlife black marketeers poach these animals for repulsive humans who will pay thousands of dollars to merely "possess" such trophies, regardless of who pulls the trigger!

Both state and federal laws are usually violated sometime during the commission of most crimes against wildlife for profit. At such times, state and federal game wardens team up to bring the violators to justice. Through this combined effort, many complex wildlife black market cases, some involving clandestine operations, have been brought to satisfactory closure in the western states. Such operations usually include corrupt outfitters, guides and taxidermists among others. And those wealthy and abhorrent examples of humankind who must possess trophy heads at any cost are the cause of it all!

It's all about supply and demand among dishonest people, and the illegal wildlife business is thriving.

There is also a lesson here to be heeded: Many folks in today's world are turned completely off by the "look at what all I've killed" mentality displayed by many trophy hunters. Current manifestations by game trophy fanatics pose an imminent threat to sports-hunting as we presently know it.

So that the smaller operators will not feel completely left out of this discussion, the following account is related:

One self-serving constitutionalist had repeatedly, but unsuccessfully, tested in court his notion that our Founding Fathers had somehow granted him the exclusive right to operate his car however he deemed fit and without the required license. He drove many miles on public roads, at high rates of speed, always contending that the United States Constitution doesn't require citizens to hold driver's licenses. (The founding fathers didn't mention pilot's licenses, either, oddly enough.) He was arrested and convicted several times.

On another occasion, when the old gentleman's rotten mailbox finally collapsed, he tried conning the Wyoming highway department into erecting a new one, by suggesting to them that one of their snowplows had destroyed it. After that attempt failed, he demanded that the game and fish department replace the mailbox because a deer had been struck by a vehicle and thrown against it. That one didn't work either.

Next, the old-timer prepared to challenge society's wildlife laws. He began offering hunting and fishing privileges (no license required and at any season) as an enticement to those who would rent his dilapidated and vermin-ridden dude ranch cabins. The only fee was his requirement that he receive half of all the ill-gotten proceeds. A jury convicted the old scalawag of being an accessory to taking two deer out of season and possessing half of each. The judge gave him a hefty fine and a jail sentence for the offenses. The aging tax protester then somehow used the system he so despised to provide him with a public defender to fight the conviction at decent folks' expense. The case dragged on for three years until the old rascal's conviction was finally upheld. He never served a day in jail or paid one dollar of the fine, however, because the county attorney had inadvertently failed to act within the legal time-frame after the final court decision. Only in America!

Those Damned Deer

Wyoming folks are known for their independent ways and conservative philosophies. Generally they detest government handout programs that benefit the able-bodied. The state has, however, the most liberal landowner relief statutes, regulations, policies, programs and attitudes governing wildlife's use of privately owned lands as found anywhere on this planet. And Wyoming's game wardens are charged with sorting it all out. Along with their law enforcement and game management responsibilities, game wardens are also given the thankless and usually discomforting duty of game damage control and claim investigation.

Consider the myriad of ways that Cowboy State landowners are compensated for game animal use of their lands.

First, there is Section 23-1-901 of the Wyoming statutes. This law allows compensation to a landowner, lessee or agent whose property is being damaged by any of the big game (antelope, bighorn sheep, deer, elk, moose or mountain goat) or trophy game (black bear, grizzly bear or mountain lion) animals or game birds of the state. And the law sets no monetary limit for game damage redress.

The statute reads: "The department (game and fish) shall consider the claims based upon a description of the livestock or bees damaged or killed by a trophy game animal, the damaged land, growing cultivated crops, stored crops including honey and hives, seed crops, improvements and extraordinary damage to grass."

The necessity of allowing hunting on such damaged private property is addressed in the statute this way: "No award shall be allowed to any landowner who has not permitted hunting on his property during authorized hunting seasons." Wyoming's attorney general has interpreted this sentence to mean "any hunting at all" will be sufficient to qualify for game damage compensation. So a claimant can meet the legal requirement by inviting a few friends out for a hunt.

Because some landowners wanted compensation merely for game animal use of their lands, the "Cowboy Legislature" passed an additional law placing an $11 landowner coupon on every antelope, deer and elk license issued by the state. Only landowner coupons from hunters' licenses where game animals are taken on private lands, and not on public leased lands, legally qualify for payment under the law. Each year, a number of improper coupon redemptions are suspected.

The $11 coupon represents half the cost of a resident deer or antelope license, and a third of the cost of a resident elk license. Landowner license coupons are redeemed through the game and fish department which uses license fee revenues for funding. Landowner coupon redemptions cost Wyoming sportsmen over a half million dollars each year.

The game and fish department also provides landowners with big game panels or fencing material, free of charge, for haystack protection.

Landowners may charge hunters whatever "trespass fee" the market will bear for the privilege of hunting their lands. And, landowners charging trespass fees are not barred from other forms of wildlife recompense.

Are Wyoming landowners less troubled by private land wildlife use issues than are landowners elsewhere? If the recurring concern voiced by Farm Bureau and other associations about these issues is an accurate barometer of landowner attitudes, the answer to the question is a resounding "No!"

It should take little imagination to picture what often happens when a landowner or his friend is caught violating game laws. At such a time many ranchers will attempt to hold the game warden hostage by threatening to file game damage claims, to call the governor demanding his job and to deal him all sorts of other miseries if he proceeds with the matter even though the warden has no other ethical alternative than to take a game violator through the court system.

Quite often a violator's game damage confrontation with the department begins even before criminal court is over. And whether or not the game damage complaint is legitimate, it is still likely to tie up the game warden for months with game damage control measures in an attempt to keep big game animals off the private property, as well as taking game counts and recording other pertinent information that will be needed should a damage claim be filed.

However, let it be said here that the majority of the state's landowners seldom complain about wildlife using their property. And when they do holler, they usually have a legitimate complaint. Yet others are always testing the system for ways to take unfair advantage of it. And the mere presence of such a lucrative game damage law beckons to those with nefarious motives.

A number of game damage claims are submitted to the game department each year (202 in 1997). A just claim requesting reasonable game damage compensation that has been filed in a timely fashion will almost certainly be paid by the department after commission review. The game damage program costs hunting and fishing license holders nearly a million dollars each year.

Many unreasonable, and a few unfounded, game damage claims are filed with the department. Game damage control and damage claim investigation takes untold game warden-hours each year.

One Cody area landowner had the state's "no ceiling limit" game damage law memorized.

He learned the do's and don'ts of the statute. Early one year, the guy started casually mentioning round and about that he expected to be the first person in Park County, Wyoming, ever to succeed as a commercial strawberry grower. He intended to plant five acres to the crop that spring. He even set up an appointment with me to explain the extensive investment that he would have in the plants, equipment and labor needed for the operation. The would-be strawberry farmer went into great detail, expounding on the complex and very costly science of growing strawberries commercially and quoted selected excerpts from horticulture handbooks. He went on to explain that it would take at least two years to establish the expensive varieties most suited for the climate. He said he had contacted me because the greatest threat to such a venture would be the area's mule deer herds.[1]

The fellow was aware of the game damage statute requirement that a landowner notify the department within 15 days of discovery of the damage. He assured me that such notification would most certainly be given the minute a deer posed a threat to his future operation. It seemed quite clear that game animals were going to be the cause of a future horticultural holocaust, and the department was going to pay!

It was late September when the strawberry farmer was next heard from. He complained to the district office secretary that "those damned deer" were beginning to destroy his strawberry patch, and I was immediately apprised of the situation.

Considering the source, maybe the complaint shouldn't have come as a surprise. But there had been few deer in the complainant's vicinity that summer, and the migrant herds had yet to arrive for the winter. I was soon on my way to investigate the reported wildlife problem.

I found the strawberry plants intertwined with five acres of weeds! The patch had obviously not been properly farmed. After a rather intense search, I

---

[1] While a few mule deer spend the entire year in the area's lower elevations, the majority of the herds summer high in the surrounding mountains and return in late fall to winter in the valley.

found the tracks of a doe deer and her two fawns in one corner of the field. But it was very evident that the deer family was the least of the farmer's problems.

However, since the department had received an "official" game damage complaint, it was now obliged to take appropriate action no matter how ridiculous it may seem.

A number of photos of the weed patch were taken, and a close vigil on the plot began. During the next several nights an attempt was made, with the aid of a spotlight, to determine the exact numbers of deer living near the man's strawberry patch. Only three deer – a mule deer doe with two fawns – were found anywhere near the tract. Most such frivolous complaints would have soon been forgotten. But not this one. The complainant here meant business.

It was hoped that the silly complaint was so obviously without merit that it wouldn't be pursued. Still, that possibility couldn't be considered at the time, and a zon gun (a noise-making propane cannon) was used in an attempt to scare off the poor doe and her fawns so there could be no complaint regarding our efforts. The cannon was set to go off at three-minute-intervals, 24-hours a day, for two months and would most likely disturb the complainant more than the deer. And our vigilance at the weed patch was continued.

Nobody was really surprised when the department received a game damage claim from the fellow several weeks later. The surprise was the monetary amount of damages: $52,730!

The damage claim described in great detail how deer had destroyed the strawberry crop by their constant grazing on the plants, and the loss of future revenue due to this damage was calculated out. The claim was a maze of computations. It seemed both frivolous and fraudulent.

We were not laughing, however, because all too often the department is placed in the position of having to prove a damage claim is unjust rather than the other way around, as it's supposed to be. Here, fair or not, the "burden of proof" is usually placed more on the defendant (game department) than on the accuser (claimant). Greatly exaggerated damage claims are many times allowed by arbitration boards because they tend to favor landowners over the department.

Although there seemed to be an overwhelming lack of physical evidence to support deer damage to the strawberries, we couldn't afford to take any chances. Examination of the strawberry plot by an impartial expert was needed. Since the University of Wyoming no longer had a horticulture department, we located an expert at the University of Montana's experimental farm in the Bitterroot Valley.

Wild Journey

The horticulturist made two field inspections of the strawberry patch: one shortly after our contact with him, and the other after the ground froze for the winter. He concluded that deer had nothing to do with the condition of the claimant's strawberry patch, but rather, any problems were caused by poor farming practices and a climate not usually kind to such business enterprises. The expert determined that what few plants the doe and her fawns had grazed on had been eaten after the ground had frozen and therefore no plants had been injured.

The Wyoming Game and Fish Commission denied payment of the claim based on the field investigation report and the horticulturist's findings.

The claimant immediately asked for an arbitration hearing on his claim as is provided for by law, and retained a prominent attorney to represent him.

An arbitration procedure was begun. Wyoming law provides for three citizens to sit on a board to hear a case. The claimant and the department each would select a member, and those two members would then select the third member.

In this particular case, the claimant, for some mysterious reason, selected a proficient farmer (fortunately for the state), the department selected a sportsman, and the third member selected was a high school science teacher.

At the hearing the department was represented by the Wyoming attorney general's office and the claimant by his attorney. Of all the evidence presented to the board, the horticulturist's expert testimony and the weed-patch photos were the most compelling.

The arbitration board's unanimous decision was that the claim was unfounded and therefore it did not award the claimant one red cent. This was the first time in memory when a game damage arbitration board had not awarded some monetary amount to a claimant.

Even though the case had been won, it cost the department considerably, both in time and money. Several folks familiar with the case pushed for prosecution of the claimant under a fraudulent claims statute. They argued that trying him in criminal court would send out a much-needed message. State officials chose not to pursue the matter.

Throughout the years, many game damage ruses have been tried around the state with varying degrees of success.

One winter evening a Little Snake River sheepman called the game warden complaining that "the damned deer" were destroying his haystacks. The rancher told the rookie warden that the animals were eating into his haystacks and undermining them, causing a considerable loss of money to him. He said the ground around the stacks was solid deer turds. The stockman suggested to the warden that he need only go out to check on the deer at night as the animals would not be found at the haystacks during daylight hours. Because deer are mostly nocturnal by nature, the warden checked the stacks only at night, as suggested by the rancher, for about a week.

To keep things in the proper perspective, one must first understand that our young officer still had a degree of trust in his fellow man during this early phase of his career.

Each night, more damage had occurred to the haystacks, and, although a few deer were in the vicinity, only once were any of the animals observed next to the stacks. Finally, with flashlight in hand, the warden looked a little closer at the evidence and found considerable sheep's wool inside the stackyard. And, although sheep droppings are quite similar in configuration to those of deer, the rancher's "deer turds" had been – for the most part – deposited by his band of sheep.

Inspecting the stacks the next day about noon, the warden found the stackyard gates thrown wide open and the rancher's sheep busy consuming hay. The sheepman had been purposely allowing his flock to feed on the stacks in the middle of the day, and then, before evening, he would run them off. The dishonest old stockman's expectation of receiving a "game damage" payment had been dashed.

It had been a great learning experience, though, for both rancher and game warden.

The Moose Slayers

That the primitive moose is still hanging around this enlightened world of ours is truly amazing!

Early unrestricted hunting eliminated the moose, as it did other large game animals, from much of its ancestral range in the Lower 48. Other species were re-established but poachers kept the moose from returning in some locations as far back as a hundred years ago.

Ernest Thompson Seton, in his famous book *Lives of Game Animals,* tells of the 1903 reintroduction of moose to the Adirondacks after the animals were extirpated there before the Civil War. Of the 12 moose released there, half of which were bulls, none survived what Seton called "shameless poachers" by the first breeding season.

Poachers are still hard at work, wreaking havoc with the great beasts.

Poaching continues to threaten the viability of many small moose populations in the state of Wyoming and elsewhere. Even in well-established herds, poaching denies many legitimate sportsmen the chance to hunt a moose.

Wildlife officials say poachers in northern Idaho and Washington are illegally gunning down record numbers of moose, continuing a five-year trend.

Because of its nature, a moose is extremely vulnerable to poachers. Moose are largely undaunted by humans and don't run away when approached as do other big game animals. Society's gunslinging miscreants use the easygoing animals for year-round target practice. Throughout the Northwest's moose country, unknown but significant numbers of the laid-back beasts are lost to illegal slayings each year.

Zoologist George Shiras III had for more than 30 years studied the moose on their various ranges in North America. "In that time," states the scientist, "I have seen more than 1000 Moose at close range, photographing some 200 in the daytime at a distance of from 25 to 150 feet; and nearly 200 at night by flashlight, at distances from 10 to 30 feet. In all that period, I never saw more than 4 or 5 Moose that evinced any great alarm at human scent."

Most illegally killed moose are shot by hunters who are out gunning for other big game species. Call them cases of mistaken identity if you wish, but these hunters are simply careless and inept or such incidents wouldn't occur. Some of these trigger-happy dorks just simply want to get their guns off!

It was mid-November and big game hunting season was in full swing in the Cody country. There was about a foot of snow on the ground and hunters were harvesting many deer and elk. I was busy checking weekend hunters up the North Fork of the Shoshone River when a sheriff's dispatcher told me she had just received a report that moose were poached the day before on Elk Fork Creek. The reporting party said two moose had been shot and abandoned late in the afternoon.

I was only ten miles upriver from that location, so I immediately headed down country.

I soon arrived at the scene of the crime, about a mile above the main campgrounds, with only about an hour of daylight remaining. The carcasses of two moose could be seen from the well-traveled and snow-packed four-wheel drive trail going up the west side of Elk Fork. By the tracks in the snow I could tell that a number of folks had left the road and walked down into the creek bottom to inspect the dead moose. It was disturbing that so many hunters apparently knew about the violation yet we had received only the one belated report of the incident.

As time allowed, I approached the kill sites, attempting to sort through the many tracks made in the snow since the crime had occurred. During the past 24 hours, curious hunters had unintentionally tromped out considerable evidence around the crime scene. I found a total of three moose had been shot: a bull, a cow and a calf. All had been shot while the animals lounged near some willows growing along the creek. Only the calf had been gutted. No one had attempted to dress out the mature animals and I could smell the spoiled meat.

The individual who had gutted the calf wore very small boots with an unusual design on the heels and soles. Because of the boot size, it appeared that the person was either a small woman or a young boy.

Hurriedly backtracking the small suspect through the maze of tracks, I found the spot from which the shots had been fired, on a rise near the trail. Here, I found five empty 7mm Remington magnum cases in the snow surrounding the small footprints. No other human tracks were there. After firing the shots, the perpetrator had urinated in a manner indicating we were after a male individual. He had both left the road and returned to it from near this location. But the direction the poacher had taken after reaching the road could not be determined because the sign had been obliterated by recent traffic.

Wild Journey

By then, it was almost dark. Bullets could be retrieved from the carcasses the next day. Yet that evening, the search for potential witnesses must begin. The poacher himself was likely to be long gone.

Tensleep game warden Tom DeSomber was in the Cody area helping us with the hunt, so I called him on the radio requesting his help that evening with interviewing folks in the surrounding hunting camps. A number of hunters had heard shots at dusk the night before, but no one claimed to have any knowledge of the moose slaying incident. Nor did we observe any small suspects. Tom and I agreed to meet at the main campground at first light. It was becoming quite apparent that some luck would be needed if the case was to be solved. That luck would come the next day.

Back in the area before sunup, we still hoped to find a witness, or at least a campsite where the suspect had been. I stayed on the lower Elk Fork road checking all hunters coming out of the hills, while Tom searched in the snow around the campsites for sign of that characteristic boot. Most hunters had camped on the lower end of the creek so we concentrated our effort there. We would later patrol on up country if need be. There was a good chance the poacher had not even camped at all, but had driven up and back from town to hunt only Friday.

It was now Sunday, and hunters began leaving the area for town after a weekend of hunting. We checked the rifles and boots of all hunters we contacted that morning. Our persistence paid off about noon when a party of three Cody hunters who had been camped above the crime site came out, heading for home with their camp.

One of the three rifles in the pickup was a model 700 Remington, 7mm magnum caliber. A little guy sitting in the middle stuttered as he claimed it.

As he stepped out of the pickup we immediately recognized the design his small boots had left in the snow. His ammunition was of the same brand as the empty cases found at the kill site.

The 36-year-old hunter finally told us the story. He had been elk hunting alone late Friday afternoon below camp when he saw what he thought were three elk in the waning light. He had fired a total of six rounds at the animals. He had killed all three animals so that each hunter in the party could tag one. The poacher then field-dressed the calf, but could not handle the two larger animals. The little slob hunter then left for camp to get his buddies. The other two hunters immediately recognized the animals for what they were. After that, the three dead moose were left to rot.

The little twerp only had a license to take a bull elk. The other two hunters of course denied they would have tagged the "extra animals" had they been elk. Party hunting is an illegal practice in Wyoming.

This moose slayer was fined $1700, given a 30-day jail sentence, and lost his hunting and fishing privileges for two years.

Impulse and thrill killers destroy almost as many moose as do careless and inept hunters. These sick individuals kill animals for whatever lift they might derive from such acts. It's a pretty safe bet they all shoot road signs for practice. Every community grows a few of them. And while sad, it is also true that 90 percent of the perpetrators of such acts are in the 15 to 24-year-old age group, which closely parallels that of other criminal activity.

One Sunday afternoon in early December we received a report that a bull moose was thought to be dying from gunshot wounds near the Boy Scout Camp at Kitty Creek west of Cody. The reporting party would be waiting for us to arrive at the scene.

By the time warden Jim Oudin and I arrived in the area, the moose had died. The animal had been shot in its side a number of times.

The reporting party had been looking for a Christmas tree and had heard a number of shots being fired near where they later found the wounded moose. Only one other party was known to have been in the area at the time of the shooting: two young men who were thought to also be seeking a tree because of the ax one of them carried. Although no firearms had been seen, the witness, after hearing the shots, had taken note of the party's vehicle, including its license plate number,

We followed the two suspects' trail from where they had first left the vehicle, back to their return to it. Near the bloody moose tracks we found where one of them had ejected six empty .357 handgun cartridge cases from a revolver. And from the moose's carcass we retrieved several bullets which approximated that caliber.

It appeared that the two had started out actually looking for a Christmas tree. However, things changed after the moose was spotted. Then, one of them had emptied the handgun he carried under his coat into the complaisant animal.

Armed with search warrants, we first contacted the suspects at their homes early the next morning. At one of the residences, a brand new Ruger revolver of the right caliber was seized for a ballistics comparison test on the bullets taken from the moose. Anticipating our move, the smug young criminal had forced an iron nail into the weapon's muzzle, greatly damaging its rifling so that a test bullet would be unlikely to match the others. The not-so-clever poacher, however, had failed to foul the revolver's cylinder chambers and firing pin in a similar manner. The empty .357 magnum cases found near the kill site tied the gun to the crime and the 20-year-old poacher was convicted of the dastardly deed. The concerned citizens who promptly reported the incident deserve the credit for the poacher's capture.

Most moose poachers flee immediately after the slayings and never touch the animal's carcass, but bulls are occasionally killed solely for their antlers. Seldom are moose illegally killed for meat alone because the rather lengthy butchering process of such large animals greatly increases poachers' changes of getting caught in the act.

Few things raise decent folks' dander as does the wanton destruction of animals. Such senseless killings of big game animals occur both during and after legal hunting seasons.

Never is a hunter justified in mistaking a moose for another big game species. While mistakes do happen, most such illegal shootings are caused by either carelessness or ineptness. Still, a hunter who immediately turns himself in for such an infraction deserves to be dealt with in a considerate manner. If such a violation is reported in a timely fashion, the animal's meat can usually be salvaged. It is important that wildlife officers strive to distinguish between an honest mistake and an intentional violation.

Wildlife thrill-shooters need to be fully recognized for what they are and should be dealt with accordingly.

These roadhunting low-lifes often shoot either from a vehicle's open window or from the roadway, which can make their apprehension more difficult because sparse evidence is left behind. They don't cleverly plan it that way. It happens because they're usually tanked or doped up and too lackadaisical to move far from their vehicle. Such vandals will most certainly shoot streetlights, road signs, unattended vehicles, machinery and anything else in their paths. The misfits are most often apprehended after they inadvertently tattle on themselves while boasting to others about their "cool" exploits.

Those convicted of killing animals for sheer pleasure deserve the severest of penalties and should never again be allowed to possess a firearm.

Alert and concerned citizens getting involved can help reduce atrocious crimes of this sort.

A Day to Remember

With the exception of a peculiar greenish-yellow hue to the southern sky, it was a beautiful July morning as my 14-year-old son Scott and I saddled and packed our horses for the trip out of the backcountry. We had been on a two-week-long wilderness patrol of the Yellowstone River headwaters in the Teton Wilderness.

Not a breeze stirred as we got an early start from the Wyoming Game and Fish Department's Thorofare patrol cabin. Since there was a 9,700-foot mountain pass to cross en route, we planned to take two days to travel the 34 miles out. This would also give us plenty of time to perform routine patrol duties along the way. We planned to camp in the meadows the other side of Eagle Creek Pass that evening, a distance of about 25 miles.

The route took us through a corner of Yellowstone Park, and we were making good time as we rode northeasterly up the Mountain Creek trail

Eagle Creek Pass on the border of Yellowstone National Park and the Shoshone National Forest. Photo: Dave Bragonier

towards the pass. Looking over my shoulder to the southwest, I could see the ominous looking clouds gathering force.

By mid-afternoon the mountain tops were quickly becoming socked-in and it began to spit rain. Gaining the summit, we experienced hail driven by gale-force winds and trees were crashing down all around us. There was no turning back now. Fortunately, we were traveling with the wind as neither man nor beast could face such a tempest. We had no choice but to continue through the dangerous black timber on the Eagle Creek side of the pass. Though we were now on the lee side of the mountain, falling trees continued to spook the nervous horses.

After a while the wind died down and the hail changed to sheets of water, amid great claps of thunder reverberating off the canyon walls. It sounded as if locomotives were going full-tilt in several different directions.

A bit later, the turbulence gave way to a more normal rainfall as we continued on our way down towards the meadows. So far, we had been able to get over, or around, the downed timber on the trail. The farther down the mountain we traveled, the higher the streams became. There was a good chance that we would be forced to camp in the black timber somewhere above the meadows. However, if it came to that, it definitely wouldn't be a "dry camp!"

The upper tributaries, though high, were safely crossed by our experienced mountain horses. Now, as we neared a deep, narrow – and usually dry – cut crossing the trail, we could hear a fast approaching great rushing sound, and within seconds a wall of water shot in front of us down the ravine. Within 15 minutes, though, we were able to cross the short wash as the water ebbed. It was a different story, however, when we reached the south fork of Eagle Creek. Here, we found the stream out of its banks, and trees and other debris were being swept down the cascading and treacherous channel. By now it had stopped raining, and we hoped that the stream would subside enough for us to cross sometime before dark, as there were no decent horse campsites behind us on this side of the pass.

Waiting at the crossing for the waters to ease off, I reflected back several years to an incident that had occurred on a patrol up the North Fork of the Shoshone River during the spring of the year. I had arrived at the Jones Creek crossing before the usual high-water of late afternoon that one can expect that time of year. One of my pack horses was young and inexperienced. I had a light pack on him and had brought him along mainly for the training. The water at the ford, though high and fast, did not quite reach the horses' bellies and was not dangerous. Halfway across, the colt broke away and immediately turned his head downstream. Following the swift water

Wild Journey

Aftermath of blowdown or tornado that struck near Enos Lake in the Teton Wilderness on July 21, 1987. Photo: Bridger-Teton National Forest

down the river, as a green horse is prone to do, he was soon into a deep and churning hole. The icy turbulence swept the horse off his feet and started rolling him downstream to the other side of the river. Spurring my riding horse on across the stream with the other packhorses, I raced down the bank and caught up with the distressed horse. I then foolishly plunged into the stream on foot to try, somehow, to help the panic-stricken colt. Amid his frantically thrashing hooves, I tried to hold his head above the water, to no avail! The force of the water made it impossible for me to do anything to help save the powerful animal. I am probably lucky to be able to tell about it today. The whole thing was over in seconds, along with my plans for this good young horse. Horses give up very quickly in a tight spot, seemingly from shock as much as anything.

As I knelt next to the horse's carcass, washed ashore some distance downstream, I found it difficult to believe the gelding was gone. The horse's inexperience had more to do with the tragedy than did the crossing. Still, I thought of crossings I had made when the sounds of churning boulders were coming from the waters. Never again. I had undoubtedly been counted among the many fools that the Good Lord often protects. I had vowed on the spot to have more respect for all streams in the future.

Back on Eagle Creek, about sundown, the water had subsided enough for us to safely cross. By the time we arrived at my favorite campsite, we were ready to call it a day.

Wild Journey

We spent most of the next day cutting blowdowns out of the trail, and detouring around washed out areas. Finally, about dark, we arrived at the North Fork highway west of Cody.

Upon reaching the front country we heard about the destruction that the storm had caused in the country we had left that first morning. A tornado, blowdown or a micro-burst – depending on the authority cited – had leveled an area along a path 20 miles long and two miles wide with its epicenter near Enos Lake. This rare high-mountain occurrence had affected about 14,000 acres of wilderness from Box Creek northward across Two Ocean Plateau, to the Falcon Creek drainage, and ending near the mouth of Lynx Creek in the park, about a mile from where we had passed just ahead of it. The great salvo had then continued on its northeasterly course towards Eagle Creek Pass, although considerably abated by then. The storm's destruction had isolated several campers in the Enos Lake area where entire stands of trees had been blown across the trails. Luckily, the campers had time to position themselves in open meadows during the tempest and, amazingly, no one was seriously injured.

We were fortunate that July day in 1987.

Burn, Baby, Burn

A freak high-country tornado had leveled trees for 20 miles in the Teton Wilderness the year before. Now, the area was in the midst of the worst fire season on record. High summer winds joined the drought of 1988, and the many "let-burn" fires spread rapidly through the abundant fuels of the forests. By the end of July, the fires had already consumed a large portion of the 1.38 million acres that would be ravaged in the Greater Yellowstone area that year.

Mink-Huck Fire in blowdown area in 1988. Photo: Bridger-Teton National Forest.

My son Scott and I were back in the area on game patrol. We had just ridden over to the U.S. Forest Service's Hawks Rest patrol cabin to find out the latest information on the fires from wilderness ranger Ray Wilson. On the way over, we noticed the tracks of elk and bear (both grizzly and black) made the night before as the animals fled the fires. During the night, The Mink Creek fire, started by lightning ten days earlier, had raged easterly down Atlantic Creek pushed by the strong prevailing west winds.

As we visited with the ranger in front of his cabin, the fire was nearing the western edge of the mile-wide Yellowstone Meadows. He told us that a helicopter had dropped off a team of "fire behavioral experts" in the brown meadows earlier that morning to verify their prediction that the fires would never cross the meadows. Now, as we watched, the fire shot across the parched meadows with the "experts" directly in its path! They escaped the inferno only by racing to one of the few bogs that remained damp and covering themselves with their fire shelters. The Forest Service had been fighting the fire on its southern flank for some time and they now deployed firefighters along the Yellowstone River in hopes of keeping it from crossing the stream. That very day, the National Park Service had finally decided it was time to abandon its "let burn" policy in favor of active fire suppression.

By this time, the rangers from both federal agencies had removed their horses to the front country so they wouldn't be hampered with their presence as they fought to save their administrative sites, a struggle which now seemed imminent. We planned to leave for the road with our four horses early the next morning. Federal restrictions banning the use of motorized equipment in wilderness areas had been lifted during the fires. My plans were to return, with a couple of other wardens, by helicopter in an attempt to save the

Wyoming game and fish department Thorofare patrol cabin as fires approach in July, 1988. Photo: Dave Bragonier

Wild Journey

Wyoming game and fish Thorofare patrol cabin in the Teton Wilderness, before the '88 fires. The cabin was built in 1955, before the area's wilderness designation. Photo: Dave Bragonier

Wyoming Game and Fish Department's Thorofare patrol cabin. The administrative structure, built before the area's wilderness designation, is a welcome sight to wardens patrolling this vast game country.

By sundown, the fires had denuded the east face of Two Ocean Plateau south of Falcon Creek, and were burning on the banks of the Yellowstone River at Bridger Lake, about three miles from our cabin. Scott and I hit the sack early, anticipating leaving at first light.

Just before midnight we were awakened by the suffocating smell of heavy wood smoke and leaped out of bed to find a stiff west wind blowing the fire directly towards us! The wall of flames appeared to be no more than a mile distant. By 2:00 a.m., we had caught and packed our horses and were on the Yellowstone River trail headed for Eagle Creek Pass. We felt sure that we would never see our beloved little cabin again.

Arriving back in Cody, I immediately called Blackrock Ranger Station to find out the status of the fires. I was told that the crews had pretty much contained the fire at Bridger Lake and had prevented it from crossing the river to the east. Forest ranger Dennis Smith assured me that his agency would keep a close watch on the situation and deploy firefighters to our cabin-site if needed and I would not need to return. Park ranger Dave Phillips, headquartered at the nearby historic Thorofare Ranger Station, had promised me that he would keep the gasoline engines running the sprinklers to keep our cabin wet while any threat remained.

Wild Journey

Because the fire on the upper Yellowstone River had not been completely extinguished, gale-force winds sparked it anew a month later. Embers from Yellowstone Point blew across the river near Haecker's outfitter campsite, and shortly the fire was reborn and raging across Hawks Rest Mountain and into the Thorofare River drainage near the game and fish cabin.

The phone rang at the Cody warden station the smoky evening of August 25 as I sat down at the supper table. It was Alice from Lake Ranger Station in the Park. She advised me that chief ranger Dan Sholly had just reported from a reconnaissance helicopter that the game and fish cabin had just burned down and that there was nothing but smoke and flames left in the area! I cussed the Forest Service for not completely extinguishing the Yellowstone Meadows fire when they had the chance a month earlier. I clearly remember being taught as a young fireguard on that forest that you put all forest fires "dead-out." Furthermore, why hadn't they been there at the cabin, saving it as they had promised? I repeatedly tried calling Blackrock for over an hour only to get busy signals. Boy! I couldn't wait to give them a piece of my mind! I finally stayed off the phone long enough for Alice to reach me again with good news. Ranger Sholly had flown back over the site after the smoke had cleared, and found the cabin still standing!

I found out later there had been a crew stationed at the cabin. At one time during the firestorm, they had been forced to lie down in the little spring next to the cabin to keep from being burned. Those brave firefighters had risked their lives to save the structure. Thank goodness the phone was busy that evening. And, the cabin may well have been lost if it hadn't been for ranger Phillips' efforts at keeping the cabin "wet-down" all summer. Many thanks to both Dave and Dennis!

While the mountains burned, scientists everywhere were proclaiming the fires the greatest natural event in our lifetime. Yellowstone Park's chief naturalist told a concerned public, "There is no down-side to the fires. Few small animals and no large ones are being killed by the fires. This glorious event will be the rebirth of the Park!" And as firefighters were risking their lives to save both public and private property, another elated government ecologist busied himself shouting, "Burn, baby, burn!" Other scientists joined in celebration and were most certainly experiencing massive orgasms – as do pyromaniacs – as they strutted in the smoke. One pompous "expert" actually seemed to be suggesting that he had discovered that fire was a natural occurrence!

Those who lost personal property, a favorite campsite, or watched as the inferno devoured everything in its path didn't attend the celebration.

Of course fire is important in the natural scheme of things. But the '88

Wild victims of the 1988 Clover-Mist fire, North Fork of the Shoshone River. Clockwise from top left: Mule deer buck, black bear and bull elk. Photos: Tim Fagan

fires were burning too much country all at once. People were confused with all this expert rhetoric. Now, they were being told how great fire is. At other times, they had been warned about how terrible it is. For over 50 years the world's foremost authority on fire, Smoky the Bear, has been telling folks to be careful with flames while in the woods, saying, "Only you can prevent forest fires!" Which message should the public embrace?

Throughout the summer, there had been numerous reports from fire-fighters and others of charred remains of big game animals in the aftermath of the fires. Nonetheless, Yellowstone Park's chief researcher told the news media on September 16, "There have been no documented cases of large animals such as grizzlies or elk killed by the fires."

It seemed only logical to assume that animals had been lost during the many firestorms. Since most of the fires had now cooled down, the Wyoming game and fish wardens in the Cody area felt obligated to have a look for themselves. Because Wyoming's big game hunting seasons had just started, they would have little time to check out the territory. Outside the park, they wanted to census a portion of the North Fork of the Shoshone River, and parts of the Sunlight-Crandall drainages. The two areas had been hard hit by the Clover-Mist fire. The wardens were also concerned about the possible loss of elk in the Cache Creek tributary of the Lamar River in Yellowstone National Park. Here, an exceptionally wicked firestorm had devastated the landscape, and thousands of elk summered in the area. The state of Wyoming had a vested interest in these elk as its sportsmen hunt the animals in Sunlight Basin where the herds winter. A request by the game and fish for permission to inspect the Cache Creek drainage was bluntly denied by park officials. The department was told that any "looking" in the park would be done by National Park Service personnel.

The wardens proceeded to survey the two target areas outside the park, using Wyoming National Guard helicopters, and game and fish and Forest Service personnel. The survey group was divided into two and three-man teams. The teams worked on the project for a total of six days. Because of stringent safety guidelines established during the fires by the Federal Aviation Administration and the Forest Service, the teams could spend only about four to five hours each day on the ground. They quickly discovered that charred animals are not easily detected from the air and the majority of the carcasses were located by the ground crews. Bears had moved into the carnage sites to feed on the carcasses and added an element of danger to the operation.

Even so, the wardens were able to document the deaths of 81 large animals, and numerous smaller ones. The teams recorded the loss of 53 elk, three moose, four black bear and four mule deer during the hasty and very inadequate spot census. Shortly thereafter, game and fish personnel from the Jackson office surveyed a small portion of the Huck-Mink fire site and found the carcasses of 30 elk, six moose, and 13 mule deer. In addition to the mammals found on the Cody side, our fisheries personnel determined that a ten-mile stretch of the North Fork of the Shoshone River was completely devoid of trout. The fish had died from the high water temperatures caused by the fires. The heat had been so intense that it shattered boulders in mid-stream and caused great damage to the stream banks.

If the National Park Service did any kind of survey to determine loss of wildlife due to the fires, it remains a well-guarded secret. However, a party of tourists did find almost 100 scorched elk carcasses in a charred Park ravine. Word has it that the hikers had to physically drag the chief naturalist to the site in order to prove to him that wild critters really do perish in forest fires! Thereafter, all unauthorized off-road travel was restricted in the Park for the remainder of the year.

In his book, *Yellowstone and the Fires of Change*, George Wuerthner reports that, "Only 254 large animals were killed by the fires and most died from suffocation." How did Wuerthner determine this exact mortality? It seems incredible that the tourists and game wardens found 84 percent of the total fire-caused big game mortality – and with just a little effort – while searching less than one percent of the 1.5 million acres scorched by the fires. And is it more comforting to know animals may "suffocate" rather than "burn" to death?

Let's stop hoodwinking people into believing that the monstrous Fires of '88 didn't have a "down side." Immense old-growth forests, needed for biodiversity, were lost. The extremely hot firestorms consumed all organic matter on thousands of acres, including the seed-bearing cones of the conifers essential for rebirth of the forests. Vast stands of whitebark pines, an important element in healthy grizzly habitats, were destroyed. And, the high-altitude tree will not produce nuts the bears relish until it is 150 years old!

The fires did not receive four-star ratings from all scientists. A recent study, completed by Dan Tylers, a biologist for the Forest Service, found that the great loss of subalpine fir and old growth forests will deprive moose of both food and shelter during the critical winter months. "It may take at least a century for nature to replace what the fire took away," Tylers said.

The typical forest fire creates the much-touted "mosaic pattern" burn. This comparatively cool burn leaves islands of live timber untouched, producing diversity in the ecosystem. However, many of the '88 fires were not typical burns.

Let's face it: 1988 was not a very good year in the mountains.

The Riddle of
Yellowstone's Lake Trout

The rumors were true: Lake trout do indeed reside in Yellowstone Lake!

In July of 1994, Yellowstone National Park rangers confirmed that several of the trout had recently been caught by fishermen in the big lake. This was a frightening discovery. Introduction of the non-indigenous Lake or Mackinaw trout here could lead to an ecological disaster to the last stronghold of naturally occurring Yellowstone cutthroat trout as well as to the other species that are dependent on them.

There had been scattered reports of the non-indigenous trout's existence in the lake for decades. Park officials had discounted them as unlikely. Now, they offered a $10,000 reward for information leading to the arrest and conviction of whoever may have released the trout into waters of the Yellowstone River drainage.

In February of 1995, an elite group of scientists met to ponder the Park's lake trout dilemma. The discussion centered around two major issues: the feasibility of eradication of the trout from the Yellowstone River drainage and the impact that various methods of extirpation might have on the Park's natural resources. The experts were a pessimistic lot upon adjournment of the confab. Consensus had been reached on one issue, that it was most likely impossible to eliminate Lake trout from the drainage without doing a large amount of other damage to the habitat.

As soon as the ice went out that spring, gill netting was implemented to help determine the magnitude of the problem. The netting results showed the problem to be much greater than first suspected.

There had been speculation that helicopters used to haul water during the 1988 fires may have inadvertently dumped lake trout in the Yellowstone River drainage. The idea, though, was scuttled after biologists caught a 21-pound female nearly 20 years old among 150 other lake trout netted during the summer of 1996. This tended to show that the fish's presence in the lake predated the fires. Park authorities then returned to their original "illegal release" theory as the most likely cause of the tragedy.

In 1872, at the time Yellowstone became the nation's first park, the only

Photo: Dave Bragonier

trout species indigenous to the area was the Cutthroat, also called the native trout.

From 1886 until 1916, the U.S. Army administered the Park. Perhaps the sporting army officers from back East envisioned that the aggressive lake trout would be an exciting addition to the park's waters.

Lake trout were first introduced into Wyoming waters in 1890. In August of that year, fingerlings from Michigan were brought by rail to Montana. Then, from the railhead, army wagons and packhorses were used to reach the waters to be planted. The young Lake trout were released into the waters of Shoshone and Lewis Lakes.

Trout from these plants eventually found their way downstream to Jackson and Jenny Lakes. It is likely that fish from the original plant also found their way up the Snake River to populate Heart Lake. By 1906, fishermen were catching 15-pound Mackinaws in Jackson Lake.

The unwanted fish may well have been illegally introduced into Yellowstone Lake by someone. There are, however, natural scenarios for the introduction of lake trout into that drainage.

Heart Lake's feeder streams head within a stone's throw of the Yellowstone drainage. Fish-foraging birds using the area include the bald eagle, osprey, pelican, and several species of gulls. It's conceivable that an occasional bird catches a Lake trout and drops it a short distance away, into waters of the Yellowstone River drainage. Such natural events need not occur often over several decades to start things rolling. Another likely explanation exists.

In March of 1995, a *Billings Gazette* article reported that "there are no natural routes for the foreign species to reach the lake." That is an incorrect statement.

Such a route does exist south of the Park within the Teton Wilderness. At "The Parting of the Waters" on Two Ocean Pass a fish can actually swim across the Continental Divide!

I first visited the site as a young Forest Service fireguard back in the late 1950s. Two Ocean Creek, flowing south off Two Ocean Plateau, separates on a gentle rise, creating Atlantic and Pacific Creeks. This natural phenomenon is the only one of its kind in North America. Bill Daniels had related to me the story of Jim Bridger's discovery of this wonder back in the early 1800s and of the mountain man's "watchin' fish swimmin' over the mountain!"

I have revisited the place many times since that day long ago, and have never tired of it.

As game warden, I have checked the creels of many anglers on the headwaters of both the Yellowstone and the Snake rivers during the past 35 years. I have on occasion examined cutthroat trout, caught on the Yellowstone side of the pass, which displayed Snake River race characteristics and vice versa. The variety of trout native to the Snake River, the Salt River, and Grey's River, is distinctively fine-spotted when compared to the Yellowstone cut-

"Parting of the Waters" on the Continental Divide in Teton Wilderness. Photo: Dave Bragonier

throat. The cutthroat that populates Yellowstone Lake has spots below the lateral line on one side of the body numbering from less than 20 to about 110, while specimens from the Snake River have hundreds of spots below the lateral line. However, DNA testing reveals no genetic difference between the two trout populations. This all seems to suggest a subtle movement of trout across the Continental Divide, perhaps for eons.

James R. Simon, Wyoming's state fish warden during the 1940s, believed the cutthroat trout of the Snake River and the Yellowstone drainage to be the same variety. In his October 1942 *Wyoming Wildlife* article "Divided Waters" he wrote, "It is significant in this case that the native trout of the Snake River and the Yellowstone drainages are identical. It is also significant from the standpoint of fish stocking that trout can and do actually at present pass over the Continental Divide by way of a natural channel through Two Ocean Pass." On August 7, 1942, Simon reported Two Ocean Creek above the forks was flowing approximately five second-feet of water. Of this, about three second-feet turned northeast at the fork, and started on its way to the Atlantic Ocean; two second-feet turned south toward the Pacific.

If cutthroat trout can occasionally "swim over the mountain," so can lake trout!

Although lake trout are fall spawners, the younger members of the species do occasionally, for some reason, run up streams many miles during the spring high water. The event has been documented numerous times in the Buffalo Bill Reservoir population. Here, during the spring run-off, the two and three pound trout will sometimes migrate up the North Fork of the Shoshone River as far as Middle Creek near Yellowstone's East Gate, a distance of over 40 miles!

Because lake trout also thrive in streams, its other name, "Mackinaw," better fits the fish.

It is possible that lake trout from Jackson Lake – after going over the spillway of the dam and into the Snake River – have migrated up the 30-odd water-miles of Pacific Creek to Two Ocean Pass, and on over into the Yellowstone River drainage. While such an occurrence is not likely to be commonplace here, it is nonetheless feasible. An occasional lake trout, or a small school of them – when natural conditions favored the event – would be all that it would take.

Could it be that the species is now emerging, after years of piecemeal natural introduction?

Resource managers must remain cognizant of all the potential avenues open to possible introduction of non-indigenous species into Yellowstone waters. Other exotic surprises may await!

Talk about Grizzlies

What Have We Done
to the Grizzly Bear?

From the hill, the trappers could tell that they had caught a bear. In the early-morning light they could see the closed door of the culvert trap. Sometime during the night, the bear had been lured from a distant ridge by the unnatural scent of the bait – a slab of bacon – which hung on the trap's trigger mechanism.

The trappers, seasonal technicians with the Interagency Grizzly Bear Management Team hurried silently to the trap site.[1] As the humans arrived at the trap, the captured bruin could be heard frantically striking and lashing out with tooth and claw at the steel bars preventing its escape back to the wild. A grizzly bear – classified a threatened species in the lower 48 states under the federal Endangered Species Act – had been captured.

The fresh mountain breezes mingled the pungent odor of the carnivore with the fragrance of Lodgepole pine, as the team – a lead technician and her two helpers – hastily began preparing for the collection of data and radio-collaring of the bear. The leader, a graduate student, readied a drug dose to sedate the bear for the handling procedure. The drug would cause paralysis in the bear, but not unconsciousness, so the animal's senses would not be greatly inhibited. There was a loud "pop" and the capture gun's dart began releasing its tranquilizing fluid into the bear.

After a 30-minute wait, the bear still reacted to the humans and it became apparent that the dosage had been insufficient to incapacitate the 400-pound boar. The team members prided themselves, however, that it had not been an over-dose, and a dead bear. The lead trapper knew from experience how easily that can happen.

Another loud pop punctuated the air and soon the large animal succumbed and the crew began their routine. One of the technicians would record the information during the process. Another crew member started

---

[1] The IGBMT is the research arm of the Interagency Grizzly Bear Committee (IGBC). The committee is made up of representatives from the U.S. Fish and Wildlife Service, U.S. Forest Service, National Park Service, and the states of Wyoming, Montana and Idaho.

extracting a small tooth located immediately behind the canine, to be used to determine the animal's precise age. Generally, the procedure draws just a little blood. However, this time, much of it was already present, along with broken teeth, from the bear's fight with the steel bars. At the completion of the process, the leader fixed a tattoo on the inside of the bear's upper lip done for identification purposes, just in case the animal lost both (one in each ear) of its colored and numbered ear tags, which the team also placed on the bear. A three-inch-wide radio collar was then fitted around the grizzly's neck so that its movements could be monitored. This collar had to fit snug enough so that it would not slip off easily, yet remain loose enough to not impede the animal's growth, breathing and eating. The newest member of the crew wondered out loud: "How do you determine the proper fit?" The question was ignored and remained unanswered. Now, like it or not, the bear would probably wear the collar until death. Next, blood samples were taken and an antibiotic was given to help ward off infection which might be caused by the team's activities. Last, the grizzly was weighed. The crew then withdrew to a safe distance to await the bear's recovery from the drug.

This scenario has been repeated hundreds of times in Wyoming and Montana since the 1960s. Mostly, the actors were well-intentioned field

Interagency Grizzly Bear Management Team working on a tranquilized grizzly bear on Blackwater Creek in the Shoshone National Forest. Photo: Dave Bragonier

biologists, professors, college students and others, all sincerely dedicated to the survival of the bear. But, as the relentless and overwhelming activity proceeded at a breakneck pace, it became evident that a few of the aspiring scientists yearned more for the recognition and notoriety connected with "grizzly bear research," than they did for the actual welfare of the species. The one thing that all had in common was that they were "experimenting" with the grizzly.

This large-scale scientific tinkering with grizzlies gained momentum in 1975 after the bear was listed as "threatened" under the Endangered Species Act. A "no-holds-barred" mentality prevailed during this era of grizzly research, and several teams of trappers were at work in the two-state area during most years. Granted, a wealth of knowledge was gained about the great bear, but it is overshadowed by the potential damage that likely was done to the species through the "hands-on" study techniques used to gather the information.

In the early years of this rush to study the grizzly bear using hands-on methods, there were warning signs that all was not well in bear country.

Over the years mankind has been conditioning bears to humans through various means. Sloppy camping practices, using bait when hunting the animal, and the open garbage dumps utilized for many years in our parks and elsewhere, have all contributed to this habituation.

Now though, a conditioning cause had been added, albeit inadvertently, to the list that dwarfed all others: the man-handling of conscious bears by scientists. The development of atypical characteristics now being displayed in the species, such as preying on humans, parallel modern-day grizzly bear research.

Throughout the years, there have been many testimonials by knowledgeable men as to the character of the grizzly. None deny that the bear can be ferocious at times, and will fight to the finish if necessary. This ferocity in the past, though, seems to have been displayed only when the animal was wounded, surprised, cornered or protecting its young. Numerous tributes to the bear came at a time when there were many of the great beasts. The tributes came from men – hunters, explorers and scientists – who had very extensive first-hand knowledge of them.

Let's hear some of that expert testimony – from out of the past – about the grizzly bear of yesteryear:

> "Notwithstanding the sinister reputation that has won for him
> the name horribilis, grisly, ferox, etc., the Grizzly, according to all
> the best authorities, never attacks man, except when provoked. That
> is, he is a harmless, peaceful giant, perfectly satisfied to let you alone

if you let him alone... Virtually all records of the Grizzly attacking man have been in self-defense, when goaded to madness by wounds, etc. This statement finds a sort of inverted support in the widespread and apparently well-founded idea that the Grizzly never molests a sleeping man." – Ernest T. Seton, zoologist & writer.

"I have never known of a single instance where one of these bears turned out of his way, unprovoked, to attack a human being...But that they habitually seek trouble when they can avoid it, or that they ever did, I do not believe ... Of course, in judging bears, one must take into consideration the view-point of the bear. A mother with cubs who charges an intruder approaching too close to her; a sleeping bear over whom a man stumbles in a wood and who strikes him down – these must be given the benefit of their own doubts." – William H. Wright, hunter, writer and photographer.

"Nearly everyone whom a grizzly has killed went out with the special intention of killing a grizzly ... the majority of people who hold the opinion that he is not ferocious are those who have studied him without attempting to kill him; while the majority who say that he is ferocious are those who have killed or attempted to kill him." – Enos Mills, hunter, writer and naturalist.

"The grizzly's temper is defensive, not aggressive; and, unless the animal is cornered, or thinks he is cornered, he always flees from man." – Dr. Wm. T. Hornaday, zoologist, hunter and writer.

"Notwithstanding the formidable character of the Bear, we have not made use of any precautions against their attacks, and although they have been several times prowling about us in the night, they have not evinced any disposition to attack us at this season." – Major Stephen H. Long, explorer, writing about camping in grizzly country in 1820.

"Bears are nobody's fools, and they know enough to let men alone as a general thing unless they are wounded, or cornered, or have cubs ... why they never tackle a fellow when he is asleep I never could understand. They could gobble us mighty handy, but I suppose it's nature to respect a sleeping man." – David Brown, the bear hunter of the Yosemite.

More recently, Andy Russell, big game outfitter, naturalist and writer, had just published his popular book, *Grizzly Country*. Russell had lived with, and studied, grizzlies his entire life within the Waterton-Glacier parks ecosystem in Montana and Canada. In his book, Russell agrees with the assertion that grizzlies will not eat human flesh, noting, "For the smell of man in a grizzly's nose is disgusting almost to the point of nausea; but there might be extenuating circumstances."

In August of 1967, something happened to make learned men take another look at the temperament of the grizzly at a time when there was great concern for the drastically shrinking grizzly bear population in the lower forty-eight states. A number of the large predators became very aggressive and extremely vicious, seemingly without provocation. Worse yet, they began to stalk and kill humans, then *scavenge* the remains, for the first time in recorded memory!

For the first time ever in Glacier National Park, a human was killed by a grizzly bear. Ironically, two young women were killed by different bears, and at separate locations in the park; and stranger yet, it happened on the very same night: August 13, 1967.

The ink had barely dried on the first printing of Russell's new book.

The bears had attacked, and killed their victims as they slept. To further complicate known bear behavior, at least one of the young women had been scavenged by the bear. The attacks had been unprovoked and of a predatory nature. News of these gruesome attacks stunned the scientific world. What in God's name had caused such a terrible thing to happen?

"It must have been some natural phenomenon that had triggered the bears' behavior – such as a meteor shower or lunar eclipse," one expert exclaimed. "Maybe it was caused by the dry lightning, or the many wild fires that are occurring in the area!" speculated another authority.

Some zoologists felt that the attacking bears had been habituated by dirty campers. Others were sure that the attacks had been caused because the women were menstruating at the time. Still other scientists, with much less imagination, fell back on the ancient and timeworn rhetoric for any unusual bear behavior: "It was a poor pine nut and berry year!"

There were problems with all of the explanations given by the different experts for the vicious attacks. All the possible causes mentioned have been occurring since the first man met the first grizzly bear. And, man has been sleeping on the ground – alongside of woman – in dirty camps, and in grizzly country, since time immemorial, without much trouble. That is, until 1967.

Prior to 1967, Yellowstone Park had recorded only two bear-caused human fatalities since establishment in 1872. One fatality had occurred in 1906, and the other in 1916.

But, from August 1967 through May 1998, a minimum of 14 humans have been killed by grizzly bears in the two ecosystems – ten in Glacier, and four in Yellowstone. Of these, at least eight of the deaths were unprovoked, with the victims sleeping in camp at the time of the attacks and eleven of the victims had been scavenged (fed on). Predatory attacks on humans? Unheard of until 30 years ago! What could have happened to the grizzly bear for the first time ever, and during this time-frame? One development comes to mind immediately.

Again, paralleling perfectly these unusual occurrences, man had started his relentless hands-on fiddling with the big carnivore, all in the name of research and for the "salvation" of the species. But, how dare anyone suggest that the bear researchers had anything whatsoever to do with such gruesome incidents, after all that the scientific community has done for mankind!

Let's further examine the possibility that bear research is responsible, at least in part, for the behavioral changes in the grizzly. Starting in 1959 with the Craighead study, and continuing until the present time, hundreds of grizzlies have been contact-handled by researchers. Many of these handlers were poorly trained and it also takes experience to properly judge a bear's weight in relation to the drug dosage. This was particularly true with the drugs used during that period. Records show that bear researchers admit to over 50 grizzly bear mortalities due to drug overdoses alone. How many more animals should be added to that number?

The drugs commonly used during the first 30 years of bear research did not cause unconsciousness in the bears. The preferred bear drugs back then were Sucostrin and Sernylan. Sucostrin acts through the central nervous system to relax the muscles and Sernylan (phencyclidine), known in the drug culture world as PCP or "Angel Dust," functions as a sedative or tranquilizer. Remember, grizzlies under the influence of these drugs remained conscious and cognizant of their senses during the entire handling process.

Those questioning the wisdom of using Sernylan in bear research – as did a Billings science teacher – were met with fierce and damning replies by the scientists who proclaimed they had determined "Angel Dust" did not affect a bear in the same manner in which it did a human being. "Of course the drugs we're using are safe, or we wouldn't be using them," responded one of the researchers.

Ironically, many of the same scientists were vehemently chastising – and with good reason – those who were exploiting and using pesticides such as DDT, and other inadequately tested chemicals then wreaking havoc on the land.

Phencyclidine can induce a violent state in humans. Interestingly, because of the bewildering number of effects it produces in the human central nervous system, the medical profession long ago discontinued its use. And, the drug is no longer available as a veterinary anesthetic, further evidence of its ineffectiveness for use on animals.[2]

Because radio collar batteries last three years at the most, a bear must be repeatedly handled to keep the collar functioning. Many grizzlies have been drugged and fooled with a myriad of times.

I remember one such bear. First trapped with its mother as a cub, it was re-trapped and radio-collared as a yearling. Later, the novice biologist became concerned that he had not allowed for the youngster's growth and that he had probably fit the collar too snugly on the grizzly. That winter he tried, unsuccessfully, to locate the den site somewhere northwest of Cody, Wyoming, to correct his suspected mistake. Subsequently, the bear was recaptured 18 more times during its 12-year life before dragging a sleeping camper from his tent near West Yellowstone, killing him and then scavenging the remains, in June of 1983. The drug Sernylan had been used on this bear on at least six occasions. One cannot help wondering what might *not* have happened had this bear remained untouched by man.

Another sub-adult male grizzly bear was fitted with a radio-collar by the interagency grizzly bear team in 1978. He was recaptured in 1991 and the inactive collar was found to be tightly imbedded in the poor animal's neck. The grizzly had been continuously choked for 12 years. After the removal of the old collar, the bear was fitted with a new one. It was determined that the trapping team had failed to install a "canvas spacer" with the first collar that would have eventually disintegrated and allowed for the proper growth of the juvenile.

On a September day in 1994, a Casper man was hunting on the forest in the Pacific Creek drainage, just outside Grand Teton National Park. Spotting a grizzly charging towards him, the hunter tried to scare it away by yelling and waving his arms, before finally shooting it once with his large-caliber rifle at a distance of eight feet. Wounded, the bear attacked the hunter, slashing his face and breaking his arm. When the injured bear was finally located and dispatched, it was identified by its scientific trappings, and the terrible scar on its neck. It was the unfortunate bear that had worn the too-small collar for much of its life.

Grand Teton National Park had just recorded its very first grizzly bear mauling the previous month when a Park City, Utah man was nearly killed by a grizzly in an attack near the same site.

While handling bears, researchers quite often, and very naturally, scratch

[2] Most researchers now use "Telazol" to sedate bears. This drug is a combination of a tranquilizer and an anesthetic. It creates unconsciousness in the subject.

or scuff their hands during the procedure. I have watched a member of the interagency grizzly team work in the open mouth of a 400-pound grizzly boar with such a bloody hand. Just think of it. The conscious animal was able to see, smell, and actually taste a human being, all at the same time. How about that for conditioning grizzly bears to human flesh?

In the 1970's, the interagency team implemented the "saturation trapping" method for determining the size of the grizzly bear population. The concept was that when researchers started to catch more repeat bears than unmarked ones, they had probably caught a large percentage of the total bear population. For at least a couple of years, this was the research strategy, and traps and snares of all kinds were set throughout the ecosystems. Because researchers were attempting to catch and handle every bear, many older and previously wild and untouched grizzlies – the most desired and critical individuals to a wild population – were lured into these traps and took their first steps towards conditioning to man. By the end of this fiasco, few bears remained unmarked by man within the ecosystems where the technique was implemented.

During the 1980's, the interagency team chose a new strategy: they would keep active radio-collars on 30 adult sow grizzly bears to monitor reproduction. This, of course, meant continued trapping, handling and conditioning of the study sows (with cubs at side) to keep their collars' batteries fresh. New sows were recruited into the study as needed. Of course, a bear with cubs alongside is a sow. But to determine the sex of other bears, most had to be tranquilized. Therefore, it became too easy to fit the non-target boars with scientific accoutrement also. After all, they were already tranquilized. Nothing had really changed, since all bears coming down the pike were still likely victims.

So, both researchers and dirty campers attract bears to humans; the researcher when he baits his traps, and the camper with his careless handling of food. However, the researcher takes first prize for conditioning bears to man because he also handles the critters.

Habituated bears have been the culprits in most of the fatal predatory attacks on humans. Two of four human deaths in the Yellowstone Ecosystem since 1972 were caused by known radio-collared grizzlies and both victims' bodies had been scavenged.

Mother Nature produces enough deviant individuals in all species to go around, without man's help. Unnaturally aggressive individuals within a rabbit population will probably go unnoticed, at least by man. However, when the same trait shows up in a grizzly bear it soon becomes apparent – maybe not in New York City or Los Angeles – but certainly to folks who live near, or visit, the bear's domain.

Problem animals within a domestic population are usually dealt with swiftly. And a dangerous deviant trait displayed among humans must soon be confronted.

Abnormal individuals within wild animal populations are among the first to be culled by natural events such as predation, in which we'll include hunting by man. This is because the atypically aggressive, bold, or unwary individuals are frequently the first to stick their heads out of the brush.

When, however, legal hunting becomes too restrictive, or entirely banned, for the large predators that have few natural enemies other than man, the effect becomes apparent and disturbing, at least to most folks. Today, more animals within cougar and grizzly bear populations are displaying unnaturally aggressive behavior. And, realistically, little can be done about it whenever large predators are given total protection by state or federal law. Such is presently the case with the cougar in California, and with the grizzly bear in Wyoming and Montana.

The potential for dangerous contributions to the natural world escalates when mankind joins forces with Mother Nature. Nearly three decades of such joint creations are now roaming bear country with impunity under Endangered Species Act protection. Ironically, the same legislation that helped the species recover is now hampering its survival. Many grizzly bears have lost their wary, primordial, instincts. Such animals are of little value to a population. Delisting of the species would allow for more flexibility in its management. The ESA provides that adequate safeguards would remain in place to ensure proper management of the grizzly. But individual states could issue permits for the taking of grizzlies by hunters when appropriate.

Grizzly-human conflicts – in many cases leading to the injury or death of one or the other – continue to occur both within and outside of the animal's recovery area. Statistics, kept since 1982, show that these confrontations continue on an upward trend. These conflicts have caused considerable loss of public support for recovery of the species.

Grizzlies are frequenting areas where they have not been observed for nearly a century. For the first time in years, the bears are now commonly found in the Green River drainage, in the Dubois area, in the Meeteetse country, northwest of Thermopolis, and in parts of the Wind River Indian Reservation.

Between 1996 and 1998, 204 known grizzly bear cubs were born in the Yellowstone Ecosystem and just 18 known bears died. And the interagency team now has 55 active radio collars on sow grizzlies in the area, a record high.

Meanwhile, the number of overall incidents with grizzly bears is increasing dramatically as bear populations grow. The Wyoming Game and Fish Department has the statutory responsibility to investigate and pay damage claims for livestock killed by grizzly bears. In 1994, there were 24 incidents involving grizzly bear and livestock resulting in seven damage claims to the game and fish. In 1998, there were 70 bear incidents and 24 damage claims filed with the department.

According to game department figures, Wyoming has spent nearly $1 million in each of the last four years on grizzly bear management. Most of that cost went for investigating grizzly bear damage claims and damage-prevention work. Presently, those expenses are funded almost entirely by the state's hunters and anglers. Department managers expect that long-term management of a recovered bear population will prove no less costly.

The U.S. Fish and Wildlife Service, on the other hand, contributes just a small fraction of that amount, approximately $25,000 per year over each of the last four years, even though that federal agency has final authority for grizzly bear management.

The Wyoming Game and Fish Department first filed a petition in 1995 with the U.S. Fish and Wildlife Service, seeking delisting of grizzly bears within its jurisdiction. The interagency grizzly bear committee then reached a consensus that the species had arrived at a recovered level within Yellowstone and its environs. A five-year conservation strategy provided for removal of nuisance bears by sportsmen when appropriate.

Immediately, the filing set off a fervor of protests, and even court injunctions, from a coalition of conservation groups who claimed that there was yet insufficient data to allow for delisting of the grizzly bear. Three years later, lawsuits continue to tie up the removal of the animal from the threatened list.

Once found in abundance as far west as California, the grizzly's only habitat there today is on that state's flag. Mankind has greedily claimed most of the bear's ancestral range for itself.

And, traveling overnight, the grizzly can now reach mankind's outposts from the most remote corner of its domain "south of the border." Likewise, man can reach the bear's secluded niche, taking just a bit longer to do so. Most of the great bear's remaining habitat here is situated quite close to the so-called "frontcountry." Nowadays, man's presence is obvious throughout most of grizzly country in the Lower 48. And, although there is the possibility of securing more real estate for the bear at some future date, not much quality habitat remains available. The sad scenario is that there are too many people in and around too little habitat.

Wild Journey

If man and grizzly are to coexist in harmony, both must share the responsibility. Humans must conduct themselves properly while using the bear's habitat, and the bear must retrieve its wary primordial instincts. This is key to the survival of the bear species. And the grizzly's ancient trait of attacking only when wounded, surprised, or when protecting food or young would do just fine, thank you. However, the reality is that the grizzly bear is no longer the same wild animal of yesteryear!

Despite data relating to the state of the grizzly bear in northwest Wyoming and the increasing problems associated with the animals here, some folks still doubt that the species has recovered. The consequences of delaying delisting must rest solely with them. Such groups must bear the responsibility for any negative effect on the grizzly brought on by their litigation. There will always be those who oppose delisting of the grizzly bear regardless of the population level or the problems involved.

Those who claim to love the grizzly the most refuse to accept the population estimates of the experts, and demand "concrete numbers." They are sure to find a goodly supply of scientists who are eager to accommodate them. The title "grizzly bear biologist" provides a certain standing that studying the food habits of the sage grouse doesn't. It seems apparent that there are those who will not be satisfied until every bear is wearing a radio collar and ear tags.

May I issue a warning? Beware: We are loving the bear to death!

The old trapping and handling techniques will continue to degrade the species. When managers know precise grizzly bear numbers, the last of the truly wild grizzlies will have already vanished.

It becomes too easy to sit along the sidelines – like a football player's parent – and coach when you are not truly the responsible party. The bear managers entrusted with grizzly management, those who must answer to the public and deal with all real-life problems, believe that the species has reached recovery. And considering the dramatic increase of conflicts with grizzly bears outside their recovery area, one wonders just how many more grizzlies can be tolerated without allowing for a managed harvest?

The present interagency grizzly bear committee management strategy is to continue to monitor the adult female segment of the population. Female survivorship is a key factor in the welfare of the species. Hopefully, today's drugs will be kinder to the bears than the old ones were. Also helpful would be a commitment among researchers to handle bears properly when – and only when – absolutely necessary. The more a bear is handled – for whatever reason – the better the chance of its becoming a problem animal.

Researchers must stop using study techniques which require the trapping and handling of the animals. They must develop "bear friendly" research methods. Proper etiquette must be practiced by everyone using bear habitat.

The grizzly has reached a crucial juncture: It is essential for its long-term welfare that the animal's survival instinct be somehow resurrected. Unnaturally aggressive animals must be removed from the population. This will help curb the proliferation of atypical traits. Removal of such animals will also help restore lost public support for the bear, and for the governmental agencies responsible for grizzly bear management.

Let's now get the grizzly habituated back to the wild!

Humans killed by grizzly bears in the Yellowstone-Glacier ecosystems

Mo/Year Victim Activity	Bear Provoked?	Victim Scavenged?	Habituated/ Handled Bear?
GLACIER			
8/1967 Sleeping/Camp	No	Yes	Yes
8/1967 Sleeping/Camp	No	?	Yes
9/1976 Sleeping/Camp	No	Yes	Yes
6/1980 Sleeping/Camp	No	Yes	Yes
6/1980 Sleeping/Camp	No	Yes	Yes
9/1980 Sleeping/Camp	No	Yes	Yes
4/1987 Photographer	Probably	No	?
7/1987 Hiking	?	Yes	?
10/1992 Hiking	?	Yes	?
5/1998 Hiking	?	Yes	Yes
TOTAL 10		**8**	
YELLOWSTONE			
6/1972 Return to dirty camp after dark	Probably	?	Yes
6/1983 Sleeping/camp	No	Yes	Yes
7/1984 Sleeping/camp	No.	Yes	?
10/1986 Photographer	Probably	Yes	Yes
TOTAL 4		**3**	
GRAND TOTAL 14 human deaths		**11 victims scavenged**	

On the Trail in Grizzly Country

There was a time within living memory when the first question asked of a camper returning from grizzly country was "How were the bugs?" Now that question is "Did you have any bear problems?" Sure, a curious bruin would occasionally visit a wilderness camp back then, but it would always beat a hasty retreat after knocking over the frying pan. A serious unprovoked bear confrontation in the "backcountry" was yet unheard-of.

And this was during the infamous "open dumps" era when a visitor could see two dozen bears – a mix of both black and grizzly – during a day-trip to Yellowstone's "frontcountry." These garbage bears amused themselves by ripping chrome strips from automobiles and biting dumb tourists.

Roadside beggars in Yellowstone National Park in the 1950s. The cub is learning about human handouts from his mother. Photo: Dave Bragonier

Today, Yellowstone Park officials tout fewer bear-human incidents than in the past. This, however, must be kept in the proper perspective. In the old-days, "Do Not Feed The Bears" was in much smaller print on park signs. No doubt the bruins were eating a myriad of marshmallow-flavored fingers back then. A bear, though, had yet to consume an entire tourist.

Wilderness travelers 40 years ago were required only to leave a clean camp. Back then, bear country campers could bury their trash, and hang their food if they desired to.

At the time, a large portion of the region's bear population resided near the frontcountry dumps. A few wild bears stayed to roam the backcountry and mind their own business. However, the day of the bear researcher was dawning.

Until the 1970's, a hunter could take either a black or a grizzly on a bear tag. Then, a moratorium was placed on the hunting of grizzlies, and soon after, the species was declared "threatened" and was given full protection under the Endangered Species Act.

Times have been changing since, and camping in grizzly country today is definitely more challenging than in the not-too-distant past. Still, this backcountry is reasonably safe if the rules are followed. However, since enjoying the country now carries with it an element of risk, it is neither for the meek nor the trigger-happy. Those folks should not venture into grizzly country. They can do their thing in the remaining 99 percent of the bear's ancestral range, now completely grizzly-free.

One's attitude upon leaving the trailhead can play a big role in the safety of a backcountry trip. Wilderness users who believe other creatures also deserve a spot on this rock are probably going to have a safe and enjoyable wilderness experience.

You say this sounds like environmentalist rhetoric? It's meant to! Hey, for years we merely called ourselves "conservationists!" Ever hear of 'em? We pioneered the field. Conservationists have always spoken out against waste

At least 10' from ground, and 4' from top and side supports

100 yards

Sleeping Area

Cooking/Eating Area

Keep a clean and bear-resistant camp!

Used with permission. The Center for Wildlife Information, Missoula, Montana.

and exploitation of the Earth's resources. A true conservationist also adheres to the old philosophy of balancing the critters with their habitat and in the prudent cropping of a resource surplus. Simply put, it means that we care very much for Mother Earth and both Her present and future wards.

No, I'm not in the rabid category. I still shave, wash my hands, and don't wear surplus army pants. I wear leather boots, and ride a saddle made of the same stuff. I also believe that each one of us had damn well better start caring for this planet. Its equal has yet to be found. But enough of that for now.

Grizzly country game wardens are frequently asked, "Aren't you afraid of what you might run into out there in the woods?" Folks who ask that question are usually thinking about grizzly bears. However, an amazing number of naive people actually believe there is a myriad of forest denizens waiting just over the hill to gobble up all unwary wayfarers.

My life has never been threatened by any wild animal. Maybe I've just been lucky. However, ethical camping practices laced with a touch of common sense will work wonders, even with today's divergent grizzlies.

I have, though, during my game warden career, felt threatened a few times by two-legged beasts. Man is the only consistently dangerous animal to reckon with, wherever we turn up.

Anyway, before leaving for the backcountry one must become familiar with the rules. Campers can obtain a copy of the land use regulations and proper wilderness ethics, from land and wildlife management agencies. There is another prerequisite for a visit to grizzly country every bit as important as good camping ethics. One must use common sense!

The bold approach to a bear by a numbskull – for whatever reason – accounts for a number of encounters each year. Bear/idiot confrontations usually occur because of the absence of "bear savvy" and common sense. As they say, "There is little help for stupid."

"Surprise" bear/human confrontations occur because a bear's senses fail to alert it, for some reason, of man's approach. Usually, the human is traveling into the wind and the animal can neither smell nor hear the person coming. Surprise confrontations can sometimes be prevented with a better understanding of bear behavior. Humans should arm themselves with knowledge about where, when and why a bear might be expected to frequent an area.

Hikers would be well advised not to go into grizzly country alone. There is definitely safety in numbers. And the more in the party the less likely a bear will present a problem. Folks on foot might consider singing a tune while traveling in bear country, especially when facing the wind and traversing brushy or closed-in stretches of trail. Some hikers attach bells to their boots or backpacks, or even carry fog-horns and other noise-makers. While

The author on Sunshine. Photo: Wyoming Game and Fish Department

such a clamor is somewhat distracting from a wilderness experience, a bear mauling would completely ruin the trip.

There are certain areas hikers should avoid if at all possible. Never approach dead animal carcasses, and skirt areas that smell of carrion. Be extra-cautious where numerous bear tracks, scratchings or scat are observed. Those berry patches and whitebark pine stands are bear dining areas during the late-summer and fall months. Wilderness travelers need to know that passes, game trails and watercourses are favorite bear haunts.

Compliance with all regulations pertaining to food storage is mandatory for bear country campers. This may be the single most important rule to follow. Proper food storage in the backcountry is essential for your safety.

While the rules may vary somewhat according to jurisdiction, it is a basic requirement that all human and livestock food be hung a minimum of ten feet above the ground and four feet away from a tree trunk. In most jurisdictions the food storage area must be a minimum of 100 yards away from the campsite. If no food pole is available at a campsite, a tree can suffice, using the same criteria. However, it is not as easy as it may sound to find a good food-storage tree. Take plenty of rope with you. Some jurisdictions provide metal "bear boxes" for food storage, and allow for the use of approved "bear proof" panniers that can be left on the ground. I prefer hanging my food because a bear will spend more time trying to get at food in a bear box just inches from its nose and the longer a bear loiters around camp the more likely it is that there will be a confrontation.

These food storage regulations take effect during the nighttime hours and during the day whenever a camp is unoccupied.

A study done by Wyoming game and fish bear biologist Larry Roop demonstrated that unscented household ammonia seems to have a deterring effect on bears. Take some along and sprinkle it around the areas used for cooking, burning table scraps and throwing dish water. I also splash the stuff around the perimeter of my camp before retiring for the night. Its use is just another precaution one might consider to reduce the chance of an unwanted visit.

Care should be taken when cooking in bear habitat. Use one location for preparing, cooking and eating your food. Try not to distribute food scent to other places around camp. Burn your table scraps after the meal, throwing your dish water on the ashes, and then sprinkling the spot with ammonia. One should probably not take meat products into bear country. I don't follow that advice.

Sleep at least 100 yards away from your cooking and food storage locations. Sleep in clothes that are free of food odors. Perfumes, cosmetics and scented products may also attract bears.

Women are often warned that they should not go into grizzly country during their menstrual period. However, there is no evidence that grizzlies are attracted to menstrual odors, and there is no statistical evidence that known attacks on women have been related to menstruation.

Everyone going into the backcountry should keep themselves as clean and odor-free as possible.

Most of us prefer to camp near water. Bears, though, sometimes follow watercourses when they hunt and travel. Never camp in areas where you see considerable bear sign. It is more prudent to camp elsewhere and pack your water to the site, if necessary. This is especially true if you are a backpacker. A foraging bear, traveling with the wind, can come abruptly upon a hiker's silent camp. The smell of food close at hand might even tempt a wild bruin.

A horse camp is less likely to have a bear problem because of its usual noises and activity during the night. That is, considering the camp is proper. However, there can also be a bear problem here. An animal, rewarded in a dirty camp, may return to that site.

Some folks believe that horse bells attract bears. This may be true if the bear has been rewarded in such a camp. Still, I prefer to bell my horses. I believe that most bears will detour around such a camp because of the bells. Horse bells can tell you much about what's going on during the night without the need to arise to investigate. One can tell just by listening whether the horses are content or nervous about something. The gentle tolling of bells on grazing horses is music to my ears. I wake up in a cold sweat when I can't hear the bells!

You can still have a bear problem these days – even after doing everything according to Hoyle – if a well-trained bear comes rambling into your camp. I never had a bear problem, that is, until a couple of years ago.

I was returning from a two-week hitch for the game department in the

Thorofare country, and had stopped for the night at a favorite campsite on Eagle Creek. I unsaddled the horses and then, as always, made camp in an ancient grove of Engelmann spruce at the meadow's edge. After the horses had cooled down, I led them to the creek for water and then put them out for the night in the small, but lush, meadow next to camp. In the hills, a man thinks of his horses first.

I had just about finished supper when I looked down the creek to see a grizzly standing about 75 yards away. The beautiful silvertip was watching the horses and had not yet discovered me standing in the trees downwind from him. After watching the medium-sized grizzly for a while, I yelled at him. He immediately glanced my way and exploded up the mountainside. By the way he acted, I had great hopes he was one of the yet untrained and wild grizzlies left in the area.

After supper, I took great pains to bear-proof my camp, just in case. First, I hung up the small amount of food and horse cubes that remained. In the same proper manner I pulled up my shaving kit, the empty (and washed) tin cans I was packing out, and anything else I could think of that might, in any way, attract a bear. Then, after sprinkling ammonia around my tent and the cooking and cache tree areas, I retired for the night with my bear spray close at hand.

About midnight I was rudely awakened by the sounds of my empty panniers being batted around, mixed with the jangling of horse bells. I knew immediately what was up. The bear had returned to ransack my camp. Some dirtbag had no doubt trained it in a nearby campsite. Cursing and yelling, I spooked the bruin from camp. I watched in the far beam of my flashlight as the frightened bear raced blindly towards Traveler, my picket horse. The damn bear appeared to actually go under the horse's belly in its mad dash for the timber on the far side of the meadow. Now it's not that the foxtrotter hasn't seen his share of grizzly bears. It's just that he's never learned to cuddle with one. Pulling his picket-pin, the blowing horse quickly joined the hobbled horses a couple hundred yards away. The three bear-wise horses huddled together as I reset the gray's picket rope. Without the flashlight, I couldn't see my hand in front of my face. And now it started spitting rain.

By this time, I had spent an hour or so in the pitch-black – and now wet – meadow with the horses. Occasionally I would flip on the flashlight to look at the horses. I could track the bear's movements in the timber's edge by watching and listening to the horses. Now the grizzly was on the west side of the meadow. Earlier, he had been on the east side. Never was he far away, and I knew the animal wasn't going to leave soon. The bear was sure to re-enter camp the minute I went back to bed. The only prudent thing to do now was to start a fire and wait until dawn.

So, a conditioned bear can ruin a wilderness experience, whether or not you are an ethical camper. However, a camper with an attitude problem is much more likely to tangle with such an animal.

Wild bears will usually skirt a camp whenever humans are present. I have watched them, on several occasions, as they circle camp, staying in the edge of the timber, until their keen noses catch a foreign odor. Then, they quietly melt back into the wilderness and are soon gone.

This attitude thing, though, is likely the biggest problem facing grizzly-human coexistence today. Why do people who despise the grizzly continue to use the animal's habitat? Many of these pilgrims don't plan on abiding by any law – man's, or God's – when they enter the backcountry! They are gunning for bear from the moment they leave the trailhead. And when you go looking for trouble, you can usually find it. Such groups can often be identified upon sight. These folks will most certainly be on horseback and many bands will resemble "Pancho Villa's Raiders," as they will be armed to the teeth. And, at least one "bear dog" will be leading the motley crew down the trail. Those unfortunate enough to meet such an outfit on a mountain pass can only hope for lots of luck.

By the way, most dogs disrupt the wilderness scene. They agitate bears and then bring the bruins back into camp with them. They keep your camps as devoid of wildlife as they do your backyard at home. And your barking dog upsets the wilderness experience for others. I love dogs, but mine stays behind when I go into the backcountry.

Anyway, back to the banditos. These guys are the scourge of the mountains. These wannabe mountain men are the backcountry patrolman's worst nightmare. In some areas their numbers are approaching epidemic proportions. One wonders how many of these pilgrims ever have a true mountain experience. Few other folks in their proximity can. These multiple abusers usually must "exercise their rights" by shooting beer bottles with their big-bore bear pistols at least once a day.

When it comes to backcountry horsemanship, many of these bewhiskered fellows are complete zeros. If you are fortunate enough to miss a gang of these renegades while in the hills, you will, unfortunately, still get to see where they've been, usually for years to come. You can track them by the empty beer cans, bits of leather straps and baling twine strewn along the backcountry trails. Their type always leaves behind their mark for posterity. Dead trees, killed by their pawing and rearing horses, at a meadow's edge will indicate a renegade campsite for years to come. Their graying picket pins, left standing in the middle of a still hammered-out circle, will long attest to a meadow's overuse by their horses. Little wonder wilderness lovers detest these guys.

Discourteous horsemen of this stamp fit the profile of those largely responsible for the loss of horse access to many trails around the country. And they still don't get it. They just can't understand why they are being discriminated against.

Can you tell I've also had my fill of them? And I'm a horseman!

All backcountry horsemen take heed. We must all get turned around or we are going to lose the privilege of using horses on many other public trails.

It's not easy to "tread softly" when on horseback. But, we must begin to use the wilderness with more care. Let's first admit that horses are more taxing on the landscape than are backpackers.

Tying horses to live trees causes a great deal of damage in the backcountry. While this has been an illegal practice for many years almost everywhere, it is still commonly done. Trees are killed by girdling, when horses pull back on their halter ropes and by their stomping and pawing on the roots. This unsightly damage is one of the biggest complaints the anti-horse people have. Therefore, we horsemen must strive harder than ever before to use the backcountry wisely.

Backcountry horsemen should always use high-lines whenever tying in camp. A highline is a rope stretched about seven feet above the ground between two trees, preferably in a rocky location. When properly used, the high-line prevents the stock from trampling roots and chewing bark. It also allows the animals secured to it some freedom of movement. The use of tree-saver straps on each end of the high-line prevents girdling of trees. Both high-lines and picket lines need to be re-located often to prevent compacting of the soil and overgrazing. Portable electric fences work very well for picket horses, but they also must be moved often for the same reasons.

Horsemen must abide by all regulations for the jurisdiction being used. Some places now even require the scattering of horse manure.

Another common complaint that backpackers have regarding horsemen is their lack of trail ethics. They say some horsebackers have the attitude that all trails are horse trails and anyone on foot should always get out of their way. This criticism works both ways, but doesn't accomplish much.

Remember, it takes many backpackers to use the wilderness as hard as one group of horsebackers. And always keep this in mind: if it ever comes to a vote, there are more backpackers than horsebackers!

Several years back, a renegade group of horsemen went hunting in the Thorofare River area of northwest Wyoming. A member of the party shot a moose. The nimrods then hung up the quarters of meat just ten feet behind their tent and barely off the ground. This not only violated forest service regulation, but also common logic.

As might be expected, the very first night a grizzly found, and claimed, the meat. Doing exactly as the hunters had bragged they would if confronted by a grizzly bear, they shot it. The large boar was dragged a hundred yards from camp and buried in a shallow grave: the old "shoot, shovel, and shut-up" philosophy. They pulled out the next morning.

Soon after the outlaw group left the area, another grizzly bear came along and dug up the other's carcass. Then, another group of hunters, looking over the campsite, found the dead grizzly and reported the violation.

Federal fish and wildlife agents joined us in our investigation of the case. The case was solved with the help of the honest hunters and a couple of alert guides from a nearby outfitter's camp.

The case typifies numerous others within the Yellowstone ecosystem in recent years. How many grizzly bears have been killed under similar circumstances is anyone's guess.

Scents and sounds carried towards wild animals by the slightest of breezes will warn them of approaching dangers. Sometimes the breezes do not favor animals.

Probably the most common of all grizzly-human confrontations is the surprise encounter. The usual scenario is one in which a bear's acute senses failed to alert it because of a human's upwind approach. And, the stronger the wind, the greater the chance of surprising a bear. These chance meetings have no doubt been scaring the hell out of both man and beast since time immemorial.

Few bear encounters resulting in serious injuries to horsebackers are on record.

Many surprise encounters involve sow grizzlies with cubs at her side. Attacks by sows with cubs are usually of a more severe nature, and of longer duration, than are assaults by lone bears. This is no doubt because of the mother's instinct to protect her young.

A bear standing on its hind legs is only trying to understand an unknown situation. Bears in this stance are *not* preparing to attack you. You will probably know when a bear is agitated.

Laid-back ears on a grizzly bear, as with a number of other mammals, is a sure sign it is flustered. An agitated bear will most likely be "popping" its jaws or making woofing sounds, to indicate its displeasure. Actually, the hair on the back of your neck has most likely already told you there is a problem.

If a bear charges you, stand your ground. A charging bear is unhappy with your presence. However, the animal will sometimes feint an attack. Such a

An elk hunter was attacked by a grizzly bear a few yards from this day bed on Pass Creek in the Teton Wilderness. Photo: Dave Bragonier

"false" or "mock" charge by a bear may either stop short of you or the animal will run on past. Your actions can affect the outcome. Try to maintain a safe distance without running. There will only be a split second's difference between the real thing and a false charge. Have your bear spray (probably the best defensive weapon for such an attack) at the ready. And while it's easier said than done, never turn your back and run from a bear! Running may spark the bear's instinctive predator-prey behavior of chasing and catching. You cannot outrun a bear, even when scared! Avoid straight-on eye contact with the animal and back away slowly.

Explorer Major Stephen Long related an incident that occurred over 175 years ago while he was exploring the West. He wrote, "Several hunters were pursued by a Grizzly-bear that gained rapidly upon them; a boy belonging to the party, who possessed less speed than his companions, seeing the Bear at his heels fell with his face to the soil; the Bear reared upon his hind-feet over the boy, looked down for a moment upon him, then bounded over him in pursuit of the fugitives."

Much can still be learned from Long's ancient narrative, even though the major's hunters undoubtedly provoked the attack. As a last resort, play dead. Remaining in a prostrate and motionless posture is probably the wisest decision if you are caught by an angry bear. Curl into a ball, covering your neck and head with your hands and arms. Most bears will leave when you no longer pose a threat to them. Many people have survived bear attacks using these tactics. Most attack victims say the less they struggled, the less aggressive the bear was.

Playing dead, however, is not recommended if the attack is of a predatory nature. Unheard-of 30 years ago, such an attack is a possibility today. Most predatory attacks are on sleeping campers. At such a time – heaven forbid – fighting like a son-of-a-bitch is mandatory!

While "bear spray" (Oleoresin Capsicum in a solution) has yet to be "scientifically" tested in the wild, the stuff is touted by many folks who swear that its effectiveness has already been proven. This cayenne pepper spray concoction is probably the most effective – and safest – weapon available to deal with a bear at point-blank range. Its non lethal/non toxic shotgun blast range is 18 to 30 feet. I carry a canister of bear spray in the backcountry. It's kept next to my flashlight at night.

A number of hunters have been attacked by grizzly bears while hunting big game animals, usually elk. Most victims were silently hunting into the wind at the time of the attack. Some hunters manage to get off a quick, and inaccurate, shot which either misses or wounds the bear. Most don't have time to shoot. I have investigated several surprise maulings.

One incident involved a non-resident hunter from Pennsylvania. He was hunting elk out of an outfitter's camp in the Pass Creek drainage of the Thorofare River.

At the time, I was at the Thorofare patrol cabin, about 18 miles west of the location. By the time I arrived at the scene, the hunter had already been air-lifted, by helicopter, to the Jackson hospital. Federal wildlife agent Jim Klett and I investigated the incident the next day. Tracks left in the snow clearly told much of the story. The hunter's statement filled in the rest.

The hunter had started on foot from a ridge-top for the steep descent down the timbered slope to camp, about half a mile away. His guide would bring the horses down a more gentle grade. As he faced into a stiff breeze, the hunter noticed how quietly he stepped in the soft snow. The steep game trail he was following would take him just behind the horse corral.

Now he was almost within sight of camp. And then, out of the corner of his eye, he caught a glimpse of something dark racing towards him. The dusky blur slammed into him and was gone in a flash! Only as it sped away did he recognize a bear.

The hunter had, unwittingly, approached too close to the bear's day-bed. In just two jumps the bruin had struck like lightning and then left just as

Ken Heinrich assists with a dead sow grizzly bear after it was shot while attacking an elk hunter in the Teton Wilderness. Photo: Dave Bragonier.

quickly. There had been no time for thought. The hunter's rifle had been on his shoulder at the time of the attack. In a matter of two seconds, the mauling was history.

A splattering of red on the snow verified the point of impact. The frightened grizzly had most likely swatted at his adversary once only, as a warning to leave immediately, as he sped away. Yellow spots marked every gigantic leap the bear made in its hurry to flee the scene. There could be no question about it. The urinating bruin had been as scared as the hunter! And the evidence left behind in the opposite direction indicated the terrified hunter had duplicated, almost perfectly, the grizzly's departure! One can safely assume that both man and bear were unwilling participants in the event. The wind and snow conditions did not favor either that day.

Luckily, the hunter received only minor scalp lacerations He was released from the hospital after spending one night. To his credit, the hunter didn't hold any ill feelings towards the bear. He felt he was intruding in the grizzly's domain. It was his wish that the authorities would not pursue and destroy the animal.

Our investigation determined that the bear had acted naturally, given the circumstances, and had meant only to save itself. The grizzly had quite obviously felt threatened when the human intruder approached it. The bear could have very easily killed the hunter if it had wished to. We found the tracks of two different grizzlies that had been hanging around near the outfitter camp before the conflict. They had been picking on the remains of a horse that had died nearby the fall before. No action was taken against the bear.

Bear warden Kirk Inberg and I investigated another hunter mauling on the headwaters of the Thorofare River in the early fall of 1990. The incident involved a local group of elk hunters who had set up a horse camp in the area. A backcountry forest ranger, camped nearby, had called out the emergency report on her radio.

Shortly after receiving the report, Inberg and I left via helicopter for the site west of Cody. At the edge of town, we met an incoming 'copter with the mauling victim.

Upon arriving in the camp, we found the rest of the hunting party very concerned for the victim, from Cody. They had spent a very restless night comforting him and preparing for his air rescue at first light. The hunter's badly torn and bloody clothes still lay where they had cut them from him, attesting to a fierce battle.

Before leaving for the site of the mauling, about a half mile away, we interviewed the hunters to determine the facts. We were told that the victim and four other hunters had been driving a patch of black timber, on foot, for elk. Another hunter had been waiting in a nearby clearing for any elk that might be pushed his way. The hunter closest to the victim said he had heard one shot, followed by terrific screaming. He yelled back something like, "I'm coming. Hold on!" When the hunter arrived at the scene, he found the victim, still standing, with the bear pulling on his arm and the rifle. "I shot the bear while it still had a hold of him!" the hunter said. He told us he finally killed the bear after firing a total of three shots.

Arriving at the mauling site, in scattered spruce-fir timber, we found the carcass of a large female grizzly. We could detect four bullet wounds in the animal's carcass. Evidently, every shot fired at the bear had struck it. We figured the mauling victim's one shot had broken a front leg. That wound was from a different angle than the others.

As there was no snow cover at the 9,000 foot site, it was difficult to determine exactly what had happened immediately before the mauling. It appeared that the attack had taken place about 25 feet from the bear's daybed. A smaller grizzly track found nearby may have indicated that a two or three-year-old cub was still traveling with the sow. This may explain the severity of the mauling. Or was it caused by the bullet wound in the animal's foreleg?

Interviewed at the hospital, the unfortunate victim had this to say about the attack: "The first I saw, the bear was approximately 30 feet away and charging toward me. Instinct was to remove my gun from my shoulder and shoot, which I did. And, by this time, the bear had knocked me down and was biting me!" He wasn't sure, but he thought he may have seen another bear about the time of the attack.

Though severely mauled, the victim recovered and continues to tell of his harrowing experience.

The investigation determined that the hunters had been walking into a strong wind prior to the confrontation. Because of the wind, the bear's keen senses had failed to alert her of the humans' approach. It was yet another no-fault surprise encounter between man and bear.

Still, this grizzly wasn't in a farmer's hog lot. It had been minding its own business on top of a mountain and 30 miles from the nearest road. Small wonder the bear was sleeping peacefully on that ridge. The animal carried no scars or scientific marks to indicate any previous dealings with mankind. From all indications, she was one of those few remaining wild and free-roaming grizzlies, the genes of which are so desperately needed! The loss of the bear was a sad commentary on the troubled co-existence of grizzly and man.

Quite a number of elk hunter/grizzly bear clashes have occurred within the Yellowstone Ecosystem in recent years. The scenario is always similar: A big game hunter surprises a grizzly while hunting into the wind. Of the six encounters that come to mind, only two hunters were seriously injured, and they both had shot and wounded the bears. The other four grizzlies, which had not been shot, seem to have been only concerned with getting away. And this seems to be the usual outcome when hunters do not exhibit aggression by shooting the bear.

A few hunter/grizzly encounters, usually without injury, occur each year when big game hunters return to a kill-site to retrieve their meat and find a grizzly claiming the carcass. Challenging the bear for the meat could result in serious consequences. Relinquishing the carcass to the bear is the only smart thing to do.

There are many true accounts of hunters getting seriously mauled, or even killed, after first wounding a grizzly bear. However, these are merely stories of aggressors getting more than they bargained for.

In recent years, many hunters have been convicted of killing grizzlies they mistook for black bears. Most of these trigger-happy nimrods just go bear hunting and shoot the first bear they see. One can assume that many other grizzly bears have been "deep sixed" by careless hunters who shoot first and look second. And, professional guides often fit into this "slob hunter" category.

One fall, warden Tim Fagan and I were on horseback patrol in the Teton

Wilderness. At the time we were riding out of the Thorofare patrol cabin.

On that particular day, we planned to check both of the Open Creek outfitter camps. Since it would be a good 30-mile circle, we wrangled the horses before sunup. Daylight in the fall doesn't last long. Saddling the horses before breakfast allowed their backs to warm up some while we ate. After washing down a bait of buckwheat hotcakes, bacon and eggs with lots of black coffee, we were soon riding up the river in the frosty dawn.

As we approached the lower outfitter camp, we noticed a small crowd gathered behind one of the tents. Everyone was so preoccupied examining something on the ground that they failed to notice us as we dismounted and tied our horses to the hitch-rail. As we walked up to the still-focused little knot of hunters and hands, we shouted our usual, "How's hunting, fellows?"

You'd have thought the three guides had each been snapped on the ass with a bullwhip as they jumped in unison at the sound of our greeting. And immediately, most of the camp's occupants seemed to have more pressing business elsewhere. A guide, holding a knife, was left standing alone over a bear carcass. Just seconds before, the twosome had much close scrutiny. Now, the googly-eyed onlookers had moved back to a safer vantage point.

The guide, without being asked to, produced a black bear license for our examination as we knelt to inspect the partially skinned-out carcass. He related to us how he had discovered the bruin at daybreak that morning as he stepped from his tent to relieve himself. He explained how he had shot the bear which had been standing in a nearby clearing. The guide said because none of the paying guests possessed a bear license, he felt almost obligated to reduce such a handy bear to a trophy. And he played the role of a black bear slayer to the hilt, pointing to the animal's dark pelt.

A brief examination of the carcass, though, proved it to be that of a grizzly for which there was no open season at the time. It was quite obvious that the entire camp suspected it.

The silver-tipped coat of the animal was that of a "dark-phase" grizzly bear. The guy had made a careless mistake in the morning's dim light, a mistake that a professional guide should never make.

Our ten-day backcountry tour had just begun, so we scheduled the guide's initial court appearance for the next month.

This group of hunters and guides beat us out of the mountains by several days. Within hours of their arrival, Cody's citizens had heard several versions of the incident. Included was the story of a nasty grizzly's midnight raid on the camp, and how the animal had been shot in self-defense. Supposedly, the guide had then ridden all over the hills looking for a game warden to report the incident to. The townspeople heard about a terribly grueling ordeal. When he finally located a warden, he was immediately arrested for his efforts. Of course, a perpetrator's version of his crime usually jerks more tears than does the true account.

The guide pleaded guilty to the charge of taking a grizzly bear during a closed season. He was given a stiff fine, placed on probation, and had both his guiding and hunting privileges suspended.

Later that year, the local professional outfitters and guides association gave the "unfortunate guide" their annual Guide of the Year award!

Size alone is not an indicator of a bear species. There are a few very large black bears and some very small mature grizzlies. All bears begin life pretty darn little. And cubs of both species have been shot for mature animals. Many times, hunters have difficulty judging the size of a bear. A small bear standing alone in a meadow may actually appear to be rug material. Few grizzlies reach 600 pounds. Some black bears weigh this much.

Ernest Thompson Seton, in his book *Lives of Game Animals*, quotes Arthur E. Brown, then director of the Philadelphia Zoo, who wrote, "It is a curious fact in the geographic distribution of animals for which an explanation might be sought among ethical rather than physical causes...that 1,000 pound Bears are not found inhabiting the same range of country as Fairbanks scales..."

Bear identification can be rather difficult. Informed observers usually have no problems distinguishing a black from a grizzly bear. However, at times, even the experts occasionally misidentify a specimen. This is why it is so important for hunters to be extremely careful before pulling down on a bear. So, while most bears will display several tell-tale species characteristics, a few are not so easy to identify.

All too often hunters rely on color alone to identify a bear. To them, a bear with a frosty appearance is a silvertip grizzly and if the animal has a dark coat with no obvious light-colored guard hairs, it must be a black bear. While it is true that most grizzlies do have a "grizzled" or silver-hued appearance to their pelts, this is not always the case. It is very important for hunters to realize that there are color variations, or phases – cinnamon, brown, black, and all colors in-between. The color variations occur in both species and the resemblance can create confusion.

Mistakes can occur when only one species characteristic is used to identify a bear. The craggy or "dish face" is often touted for grizzly bear identification. However, mature black bears may also have this appearance. Grizzlies have a more pronounced hump on top of their shoulders than do most blacks. And black bears usually have longer ears than do most grizzlies. But, there are the exceptions.

One should use every species indicator possible for bear identification. A dish-faced bear with short ears, a frosty pelt and displaying a pronounced shoulder-hump is probably a grizzly.

Track size alone is not a reliable species indicator unless it is more than 4 1/2 inches wide, the parameters of a large black bear footprint. Obviously, this is because of the various age groups within the two populations and the atypical characteristics found in all species. However, a track made by a Wyoming bear measuring 5 1/2 inches in width and/or having 2 to 3 inch claw impressions beyond the toes was, undoubtedly, left by a grizzly. These long claws are only present on the front feet of adult grizzly bears.

The grizzly's long front claws are sometimes as short as a black bear's, worn down by the grizzly's frantic digging for rodents and roots during late summer and fall months as the animal takes on calories for the long winter. Adult grizzly toes are almost adhered together. Their tracks will show the toes to be comparatively tighter together, and more in-line, than are the more flexible toes of the black bear. So, a bear track displaying a splayed-out and curved-toe alignment would be that of a black bear.

It is sometimes necessary, even for the experts, to observe several well-defined bear tracks to identify the species that made them.

And unlike its parents, a young grizzly, with its yet-pliable toes and shorter claws, can climb a tree much like a black bear.

Used with permission. The Center for Wildlife Information, Missoula, Montana.

Most zoologists will tell you that grizzlies and black bears never hybridize. It is safer to say that rarely do the two species cross. I am aware of a few possible hybrid examples.

One was a specimen taken several years ago by a hunter during the black bear season near Jackson. The carcass was held for several days at the Jackson district office while the "experts" debated its identity. The bear was finally released back to the hunter because the animal was "most likely" a black bear.

Then there is the report of a hybrid cub born of known parents at the Salt Lake City zoo several years back. Such hybridization is probably more likely to occur in captivity than in the wild.

Here's another account of a likely grizzly-black bear hybrid. An incident took place on the North Fork of the Shoshone River west of Cody one fall. The snows from earlier storms had melted from the lower elevations, and summer-like conditions persisted. Yellowstone Park had not yet closed for the season, and quite a few of tourists were still traveling.

The story begins one early-October afternoon when the Cheyenne game and fish office received an anonymous phone call from a tourist reporting a bear incident. The man said that he had shot and wounded a bear with his shotgun the night before while camped at Newton Creek. He explained that it happened sometime during the night as the animal was clawing its way through the skylight of his motor home. After finding blood on both his vehicle and the ground the next morning, the man and his wife hastily left the area. Because the camper was afraid the bear might have been a grizzly, which he knew to be protected, he had left the state before reporting the incident. The tourist had called only because he was concerned that the wounded animal might hurt someone.

I reached the area about an hour before dark. Carrie Hunt, an Interagency Grizzly Bear Management Team member, had already arrived at the scene.

From the blood found at one of the Newton Creek camp locations, we had no problem finding the site of the incident. From there, we could follow the blood trail north across the highway and a short distance up the creek. Beyond that, however, only a fleck or two of blood were located before nighttime put a stop to the tracking.

The next morning found us back in the area, early, and with more help. Within a mile of the highway the trail petered out. Evidently the blood from the bear's wounds had begun to clot. At least the wounded animal had headed north into the Absaroka Wilderness, and away from civilization. In that direction, the next road was about 20 miles away. This would decrease the chance of a confrontation with man.

Because no distinct bear tracks were ever found, we could not determine

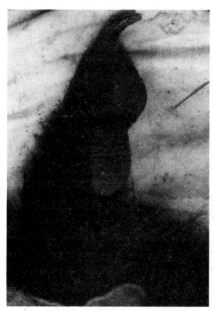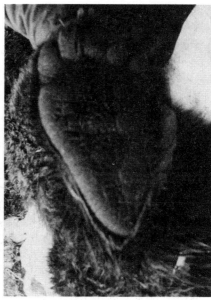

Left: side view of grizzly bear front foot. Right: hind foot of grizzly bear. Photos: Dave Bragonier

whether the animal was a grizzly or black bear. And that was the end of the story. That is, until the next spring.

In April of the following year, the proprietor of a tourist lodge on Gunbarrel Creek reported a dead bear lying in the creek below the buildings. Investigating the report, I found the extremely emaciated carcass in the middle of the shallow creek. The female bear's lower jaw and most of her tongue were missing. It was apparent that her wounds, most likely caused from a gunshot, had healed in recent months. It was also apparent that an animal with wounds of this magnitude would be unable to eat and drink.

Only a bear going into hibernation shortly after receiving such wounds could have survived the ordeal long enough for them to heal. But it had to have been a very restless slumber. Her few remaining teeth showed the bear to be an adult well past her prime. Her carcass weighed no more than 100 pounds.

It almost had to be the bruin involved in the Newton Creek affair of six months earlier. Gunbarrel Creek is the next drainage to the west of Newton Creek. The poor old-timer could no longer find sufficient natural foods, and had attempted to get a morsel from within the motor home. And the bizarre incident does not quite end here.

I took the bear's remains to the Cody district office for closer examination.

Several wardens and biologists inspected it. Characteristics of both species were evident on the specimen. The front feet appeared to be those of a grizzly. It also had the prominent hump of that species, though this may have been more pronounced because of the emaciated condition of the carcass. The beast, though, had the long ears and head of a black bear. Because of our doubts, we sent the carcass to the University of Wyoming for analysis. Curiously, I don't remember ever hearing of the necropsy results.

Now we understand it isn't always black and white, so to speak, governing bear identification. Most bears, however, are relatively simple to recognize if just a little care is taken. It is no big deal when a tourist misidentifies a bear. However, making the same mistake can find a hunter in serious trouble. It is a simple matter for a hunter to keep from killing the wrong animal. When unsure of your target, just don't shoot.

Over the years, several of the interagency grizzly bear team's radio-collared grizzlies have been found shot. The team monitors the bears' locations with frequent tracking flights. Their collars have helped locate the dead animals in various ways.

Each radio-collar has its own frequency which identifies individual bears. When "mortality mode" signals are received from a radio-collar's transmitter it usually means the bear has either died or slipped its collar. No signal at all can suggest either dead batteries or that the bear has traveled completely out of the area. It can also indicate that the bear has been killed and the collar destroyed.

The first successful federal Endangered Species Act prosecution for taking a grizzly involved a radio-collared bear. It had been nearly two weeks since the last radio-signals from the bear's collar had been received. A mid-September tracking flight had found the grizzly, alive and well, near the confluence of Open Creek with the Thorofare River. State and federal authorities were concerned because the time-frame corresponded with the opening of the area's big game season, and the radio-collar's batteries were relatively fresh.

That winter, a rumor began to circulate that a radio-collared grizzly had been poached in the Thorofare area the previous fall. Investigating the rumor, we found that most of the area's guides and outfitters had heard the rumor, but all claimed they did not know where it had originated.

State and federal game agents began a coordinated investigative effort regarding the case. Towards spring, a $2,500 reward offered by the National Audubon Society, paid off when an informant came forward. He told us that a Florida elk hunter had purposely killed the grizzly, just for the claws, while hunting with a guide along the Thorofare River.

Wild Journey

The federal fish and wildlife's enforcement chief for the intermountain region, Terry Grosz, contacted agents in Florida from his Denver office. The next day, game agents confirmed the informant's story after getting a full confession from the wealthy hunter. We found the charred remains of the radio collar and other incriminating evidence near the river where he said it would be. The hunter and guide had cut off, smashed and then burned the radio collar. After chopping off the claws, they had buried the bear's carcass.

The hunter was sentenced in a Florida federal court. He received a $5000 fine, a suspended jail sentence and lost his hunting and fishing privileges for several years.

During the investigation of the case, we discovered that one of the bear slayer's hunting companions had killed a moose and a deer without proper licenses. Both the hunter and the guide were successfully prosecuted in state court.

Without reward programs, many cases would remain unsolved. As they say, money talks.

Hopefully, one day a totally wild and free grizzly bear population will again inhabit the hills. Without them, the western wilderness is not complete.

Until then, we must be patient.

Above and Beyond

Dedicated to all game wardens who have given their lives in the name of wildlife conservation.

Murders in the Sierra Madres

In 1943, the United States was in the throes of a terrible world war being fought abroad. At the same time, agents of the Federal Bureau of Investigation had their hands full tracking down enemy agents at home. Bureau officials contacted the Wyoming Game and Fish Commission requesting its help in checking out reports that one Johann Malten, a German alien, may have been working the state for the Nazi cause.

Malten, who lived on a mining claim in the Sierra Madre Mountains south of Rawlins, was known to have served in the German Army as a sharp-shooter during World War I and although it was thought that he had desert-ed the kaiser's army, he was known to "worship" Hitler. Neighbors of the German reported the erection of an elaborate radio antenna atop his cabin, and said that he possessed a "sending and receiving set." Commissioner Bagley of the game and fish department sent game wardens William Lakanen of Rawlins and Donald Simpson of Saratoga, to investigate Malten.

The wardens contacted and arrested the 53-year-old Johann Malten on Saturday, November 27, 1943, for illegally possessing 11 beaver hides. The German also had 88 trout and some deer meat in his possession. However, the game and fish officers found no evidence of contraband or activity that might be harmful to the government.

Judge Waeckerlin of Rawlins found Malten guilty of the game violations, fined him $100, and sentenced the trapper to serve six months in the coun-ty jail. Wyoming Game and Fish Department arrest records indicate Malten was given an additional 100 days in jail in lieu of the fine payment.

Malten told Carbon County resident Joe Worth that he would kill the wardens if they ever confronted him again. Worth said that Malten had tried unsuccessfully to purchase .22 High Power ammunition. At the time, it was illegal for aliens to possess firearms in the state. Others had also heard the German make threats towards law officers.

Game warden Simpson had said that he was afraid of Malten because he had a terrible temper.

The next chapter of the story happened almost two years after the arrest

Donald S. Simpson (left) and William W. Lakanen, the two Wyoming game wardens who were murdered in the Sierra Madre Mountains on October 31, 1945. Photos: Wyoming Game and Fish Department.

of Johann Malten on poaching charges. The old German's cabin was situated just under the Continental Divide at 8520 feet. It was late fall high in the Sierra Madre Mountains and snow would be building up very quickly. If the wardens were going to check on the old poacher before winter set in, they must do it very soon.

Lakanen and Simpson made plans to leave for the mountains on Wednesday, October 31, to check on the trapper's latest activities. Snow was in the air as Lakanen left Rawlins and drove south to Saratoga to pick up his fellow warden. The two officers then traveled up the Jack Creek Road towards Malten's mining claim on Jim Creek, and their appointment with destiny. The wardens would never be seen alive again.

By Friday, November 2, two nights had passed and there had been no word from the two wardens. Lakanen's wife Carol finally called Carbon County Sheriff Glenn Penland and told him she was worried because her husband had not been prepared to be gone so long. There had been winter storms in the area, but since the two wardens were traveling together, and a number of cabins offering shelter were in the region, she hadn't been too concerned the first night. Now however, remembering the German's past threats, she feared the worst.

Sheriff Penland telephoned Frank McCary, a rancher who lived about ten miles from Malten's mining claim, and asked him to check on the situation at the German's cabin. Because it had snowed, McCary chained up his old

his Cabin on Nugget Gulch "/39.

This is the only known photograph of suspected murderer Johann Malten. Photo: Chris and Martha Larsen collection.

pickup for the drive up to the area called Nugget Gulch. He had to snow-shoe the last mile or so into the site. The rancher discovered the charred remains of the cabin and Lakanen's body, with a rifle lying across it. McCary, realizing that something terrible had occurred, wasted no time in fleeing the scene to make his report.

The rancher told sheriff Penland that fresh snow had covered everything but the ashes of the burned-down cabin and he had found no sign of warden Simpson or the German.

The sheriff left it up to his wife Sally to tell her friend Carol Lakanen the sad news.

By 6:00 p.m. Sheriff Penland and two other officers, photographer Vern Wood and a hearse had left Rawlins bound for the site.

The deaths of both officers were confirmed the next day. William W. Lakanen, 44, and a ten-year veteran with the department was a native of Glenrock, Wyoming. Donald S. Simpson, 39, had been a game warden for five years, and was born in Ft. Collins, Colorado. Both officers left behind widows, family and friends to grieve for them.

Investigators began looking for clues at the Nugget Gulch murder-site. Some now called it "Deadman's Gulch." A small stream called Jim Creek flows nearby. Two officers dug through the ruins of the old trapper's cabin, while others looked over the surrounding landscape for clues.

The investigation was in its early stages when the Carbon County coroner, Dr. E.B. Sturges, was quoted as saying, "It appeared that the trapper killed the wardens Wednesday with a rifle and then may have died in the log cabin blaze he set to hide the crime." Sheriff Penland said that he found, "the fragments of a skeleton ... one of them looked like a human knee bone." Also found in the debris were two 25-gallon gasoline cans, a .22-caliber rifle and a .38 caliber revolver.

The wildlife officers' bodies had been dragged next to the cabin, logs had been piled around them, and gasoline had been poured on their clothes. The cabin was then set on fire. Lakanen's head and back were badly burned, but the body, left face-down, could still be identified. Though the state truck was partially burned, Simpson's body had not been touched by the flames.

After studying the evidence found at the crime scene, sheriff's investigators concluded that the wardens had driven to within two feet of the cabin before being fired upon by the murderer from an open door at point-blank range. Lakanen had likely slumped over the steering wheel immediately after being shot behind the left ear, as the truck's ignition key was found in the "on" position. Simpson had been shot twice through the stomach with a .22 High Power and once in his right temple with a larger caliber projectile. He had probably received the two stomach wounds while in or near the pickup and had then attempted to gain the safety of the nearby trees but fell before reaching them. The officers theorized that the killer, upon reaching Simpson as he lay wounded on the ground, had grabbed the warden's .38 caliber revolver and shot him through the right temple with it. Powder burns indicated the murderer had leaned over to fire the .38 bullet. All cartridges in the revolver found in the cabin's ashes had been fired. Photographer Wood's photos clearly showed Simpson's jacket pulled up around his shoulders and to the back of his head, no doubt from being dragged back to the cabin by the murderer.

On Sunday, November 4, Rawlins pilot Roy Rasmusson covered the region from the air while officers on the ground searched the area in a radius of about one mile around the murder-site. After the search was completed, a sheriff's office spokesman reported, "From the lack of tracks, it is almost an impossibility that Malten escaped, but rather he died in the fire of his cabin." However, that very morning, the *Denver Post* had reported, "All tracks near the scene were covered by the recent deep snowfalls." Although it seemed a bit premature, for a murder-suicide conclusion, such a deduction would certainly be a quick and convenient one.

Folks knew it had been snowing in the mountains and wondered why the sheriff expected to find the killer's tracks in the area four days after the murders had occurred. Malten most certainly would not have lingered long after committing the atrocities. The wardens had driven a two-wheel drive pickup right to the German's cabin, yet three days later it had been necessary to snowshoe into the site. U.S. Weather Bureau records indicate precipitation had fallen at several area weather stations on the very day the wardens drove to the site.

The sheriff suspended any further search for Malten until the results of the analysis of a bone sample came back. The sample had been taken to the chemical laboratory at the University of Wyoming by Sheriff Penland the day before. Because the university's laboratory was not equipped for such an examination, the bone fragments were sent on to Washington D.C. for analysis.

Criminal investigators visited the murder site several more times, and further screening of the ashes disclosed some keys, a watch and four or five dollars in coins.

On Tuesday, November 20, the *Rawlins Republican-Bulletin* reported the following: "The local sheriff's office has received a report from the FBI in Washington, D.C. on the bone fragments, .38 caliber bullet and .38 revolver, and two pieces of flesh taken from the debris of the cabin of Johann Malten, trapper in Nugget Gulch, who has been charged with the murders of wardens William Lakanen and Don Simpson.

According to the report from the federal agency, due to the intense heat of the cabin fire, the two pieces of flesh were not in a suitable condition to conduct a serological test in order to determine identity. However, the doctor who conducted the laboratory examination, reported that the larger piece of flesh contained several pieces of bones that indicated human origin. The doctor was not able to definitely establish the bone fragments as human as they were too small in themselves. He did report, however, that one of the pieces consisted of an intact patella, commonly known as the kneecap."

The article continued, "In reference to the bullet removed from the skull of Don Simpson, the FBI, following an examination, did report that it was evidently a .38 caliber shell, but due to the condition of the .38 revolver from the intense heat of the cabin fire, they did not deem it safe to fire a bullet from the gun to compare the ballistic markings. The local authorities presumed earlier in the case that the bullet fired into Simpson's head came from his own service revolver."

The article concluded, "A formal warrant has been issued against Malten charging him with the murder of Mr. Lakanen and Mr. Simpson and the Carbon County officers will continue their investigations as to the whereabouts of the trapper unless it can definitely be proven that he died in the fire of his cabin."

The issuing of the arrest warrant for the German indicated the uncertainty of the investigators' earlier murder-suicide conclusion. Beyond this point, recorded official comment by the Carbon County sheriff's office regarding the murder case is lacking. The incident seems to have almost slipped into oblivion. Present Carbon County officials claim no files relating to the Lakanen-Simpson murder case can be found. Most of the folks still alive today who are familiar with the case say they never accepted Sheriff Penland's murder-suicide conclusion of the case. Long-time Rawlins residents say the sheriff's mishandling of the case cost his re-election. The chief investigator for the Carbon County sheriff's office assigned to the case was John Terrill, later sheriff of that county, and later still, served as Wyoming's U.S. Marshal. Terrill always defended the murder-suicide conclusion based solely on the so-called "bone fragments" found in the cabin's ashes. During a recorded interview regarding the murder investigation, Terrill mentioned attending a meeting in Cheyenne with Governor Hunt and the Wyoming Game and Fish Commission at which he explained to "everyone's satisfaction" that the murderer had committed suicide.

Archie Pendergraft, Wyoming's chief game warden at the time of the murders, would almost certainly have been in attendance of this meeting, although he was adamantly convinced that the murderer survived.

At one time Pendergraft was my supervisor, and I have heard him tell of the warden murders several times. The chief warden clearly did not buy the sheriff's suicide theory. He always said there was more evidence supporting Malten's survival than his demise. Pendergraft would say, "Why would a murderer bent on suicide need to destroy the evidence?" Since a sheriff reigns supreme as the chief criminal investigator in his county, it is solely his decision whether to request any help on a case. Chief Warden Pendergraft tried, unsuccessfully, to persuade the sheriff to request FBI assistance in the murder investigation. Neither could Pendergraft convince the governor to help in the matter. Up until his death, Archie remained convinced that he knew the reason the officials preferred not to get the Feds involved in the matter.

In his official capacity, Pendergraft had knowledge of a complex beaver-poaching ring operating within the state at the time of the murders. Although beaver were protected at the time, its fur was nonetheless a valuable commodity. Considerable black market trafficking in beaver pelts existed in the Rocky Mountain region during the 1940s. Archie believed that certain county and state government officials were involved in this clandestine activity.

Some folks say the files and evidence pertaining to the double-murder case – including the charred .22 High Power rifle and .38 caliber revolver – disappeared about the same time Terrill left the sheriff's office. The fact that Terrill's widow donated the .38 caliber revolver to the Savory Museum several years back tends to support this thought.

If the incident had occurred earlier in the war, the FBI might have pursued Malten's whereabouts after the murders for further espionage investigation. However, as the end of the war was at hand, the federal agency no doubt felt little could then be gained from any effort to track down suspected Nazi agents.

George Burnap was a game warden stationed at Lander at the time of the murders and was one of the first game department people to arrive at the scene. He had seen the so-called "kneecap" and doubted that the bone was human. Burnap thought the bone segment was more likely an elk hip-joint because it had the appearance of having been sawed from an animal for table meat. He, like Pendergraft, also felt that the game and fish department had been given the royal run-around by the investigating authorities regarding the case.

There were other reasons to suspect that Johann Malten survived the incident. The Uline family, also German immigrants and friends of Malten's, ranched on Jack Creek and left the country shortly after the murders. Malten was said to have been seen in Saratoga on the Saturday after the murders. In subsequent years, a man fitting the killer's description was occasionally observed slinking around an old friend's residence in that town.

Experts say that it takes more than a wood fire, even sprinkled with gasoline, to consume an entire human body. It takes three hours of burning with natural gas and oxygen at 1300 to 1600 degrees Fahrenheit to cremate a human body, after which the human details can still be visibly identified until the ashes are disturbed. More important, the lab tests on the bone samples were inconclusive.

A persistent rumor still circulating among senior Carbon County residents today is that Johann Malten later resided in the Grand Junction, Colorado area under an assumed name until his death and is now buried there.

In August, 1995, the Carbon County Historical Society met to address the murders. Chief game warden Jay Lawson spoke to the group. I attended this gathering. At the meeting's conclusion, Oscar Hall, an ex-prosecuting attorney for that county, asked for a secret ballot, "just for the hell of it," on the question of whether the members thought that Malten had survived the incident. All but two people of the 30-odd present thought the German had

Suspected murderer Johann Malten's cabin. Photo: Chris and Martha Larsen collection.

survived the incident! Several folks at the meeting had first-hand knowledge of the event.

There seems to be little doubt that the two game wardens were murdered as they arrived at the cabin on that fateful Wednesday afternoon on October 31, 1945. But why they left themselves so vulnerable, knowing the old poacher's demeanor and attitude towards them remains a mystery. One can only surmise it may be the carelessness connected with the security felt in numbers. This overconfident feeling when one is not alone in a tight spot has been the demise of many law officers. Also, the wardens may have speculated that by driving quickly up to the cabin they would catch the old recluse unaware. We will never know.

No one seems to doubt that Johann Malten murdered the two game wardens. But other questions persist to this day. And of course, there's the most perplexing question of all: Did he survive the atrocity? It would seem likely that he did. Did he have an accomplice? A friend may have been visiting him on the day of the murders or he could have contacted someone for assistance by radio after the murders. Because the German's vehicle was left behind, he fled either on foot or in an accomplice's vehicle. Malten had two years to plan for such an event. Not as significant but equally intriguing is the question of whether the murderer was an enemy agent. Many folks say it is ridiculous to surmise that an old recluse like Malten could have been worth much to the Nazi party at his remote location in the Wyoming mountains.

Consider, though, that the Nazi Party's SD or Sicherheitsdienst (Secret Intelligence) had already established an espionage network abroad by 1939. It was the FBI's job to track these enemy agents down, and the Bureau's agents arrested some 4,000 suspects inside the United States between 1941 and 1945. In order for a spy operation to be successful, the Germans knew they needed at least two things: safe harbors for their agents and numerous message relay stations. On both counts, how could they beat the remote location of Malten's cabin atop the Continental Divide?

Burnap had seen a radio antenna, with lead-in attached, hanging in the trees near a wicker privy, made of interwoven saplings, at the murder-site. He also stated that war-time authorities had intercepted short-wave radio transmissions of espionage significance from somewhere in south-central

The author, Terry Cleveland, and Jay Lawson (left to right) at the Sierra Madre murders site in August, 1995. Photo: Terry Cleveland

Wyoming. The source of the radio signals was never pin-pointed. Malten had a short-wave set and was overheard talking in German on it.

When just a youngster, Bob Lamberson of Rawlins visited at the Malten cabin with his friends the Larsen boys and heard Malten talking in German on a radio. Whenever Lamberson visited the Larsen Ranch after the murders he was told, "Never go to the cabin-site again. Malten is still in the area!"

Martha Larsen, 100 years young, attended the 1995 historical society meeting. She told the group that "John" Malten was both a friend and neighbor to her family. Martha said the German would often gather wild raspberries and chop wood in return for her homemade bread. She spoke of Malten's kindness and told how he would climb a very tall ladder just to place food on a "feeding platform for the birds and other animals." Mrs. Larsen believed the ladder was used solely for reaching the "feeding platform" and not to access an antenna. Martha mentioned one occasion when the German had killed a bear with an axe. She declined to talk about the murders or what she thought might have happened to the trapper. A photograph showing Malten's cabin and the ladder was taken by Chris Larsen, Martha's husband, in 1943.

I first learned about the warden murders from George Burnap while I was stationed at Baggs. He described the site and how to get there in great detail.

In August of 1962, I visited the Jim Creek murder site. It was necessary to walk the last mile because the road was in disrepair. More people had lived in the region during the 1940s. The site itself seemed little changed from the way Burnap had described finding it almost 20 years earlier. Over there were the rusting remains of a 1930's model Chevrolet pickup – and the pile of barrels – just as George had described them. The old wood stove still rested in the cabin's ashes. Even the wicker outhouse was still standing at the meadow's edge, albeit minus the antenna wire and lead-in that used to hang in the trees above it.

As I stood admiring the beautiful little meadow with its tranquil beaver pond, it didn't seem possible that something terrible had happened here. After swallowing a sandwich, I started back. Taking a short-cut through a secluded aspen patch, I came abruptly upon an image carved into the bark of one of the trees. It depicted a man's head wearing a wide-brimmed hat. The initials "J.M." were inscribed beneath the work. Those were the killer's initials! And the carvings were so fresh that an eerie sensation made my skin crawl! I glanced about, half expecting to see the retreating artist!

Sure, other folks have the same initials as the old German, but I don't buy such a coincidence here. And, a prankster would have left his design in a conspicuous location nearer the old cabin site. At the time of my visit, nearly 20 years after the murders had occurred, few people even remembered the incident let alone the old German's name. Think what you like, but I had just missed the 72-year-old son of a bitch's return to the scene of the crime!

Two other Wyoming game wardens have been slain while enforcing the law.

On September 14, 1919, assistant game warden John A. Buxton, 31, of Rock Springs was killed by Joe Omeyc from whom warden Buxton had taken a rifle for a violation of the game laws. Omeyc, an alien, then shot Buxton with a handgun he had concealed on his person. The warden's pregnant wife, who accompanied him at the time, managed to escape the murderer.

Omeyc was later apprehended by Sweetwater County sheriff John Stoddard and one of his deputies. He was convicted of second degree murder on March 17, 1920 and sentenced to not less than 20 nor more than 21 years in the Wyoming penitentiary. Omeyc was paroled on December 22, 1924, but after a parole violation was returned to the penitentiary. He was again released on December 16, 1931.

Assistant Wyoming game commissioner (warden) George Edward "Ted" Price, 31, was deputized by Hot Springs County sheriff Harry E. Holdrege to assist him and deputy Palmer in the apprehension of bootleggers Elsworth Mullendore and Starkey Powers. A tip had been received that the outlaws were headed towards Thermopolis from Meeteetse with a load of moonshine. In the early morning hours of August 31, 1921, a gunfight ensued between the lawmen and rumrunners at the Cottonwood Crossing. Price was shot through the heart by Mullendore, who then received a mortal wound from a shot fired by deputy Palmer. Powers then surrendered to the surviving officers.

Murder site in relation to nearby towns

★ **Rawlins**

★ **Elk Mountain**

★ **Saratoga**

★ **MURDER SITE**
Elevation : 8520 feet. Section 10, T15, R87

★ **Baggs**　　★ **Encampment**
★ **Dixon**

WYOMING
COLORADO

Fall, 1945 - Carbon County, Wyoming

Weather station	Precipitation by day					high/low temperatures				
	10/30	10/31	11/1	11/2	11/3	10/30	10/31	11/1	11/2	11/3
Elk Mountain	.20	.30	.20	T	T	-	-	-	-	-
Encampment	-	.09	T	06	-	56/34	40/24	42/29	51/29	60/32
Saratoga	-	.02	-	-	-	58/32	43/31	46/30	49/31	53/33
Dixon	-	T	-	10		60/32	43/30	46/31	50/32	59/21

from U.S. Weather Bureau records

Overdue

News of an overdue aircraft carrying two Wyoming Game and Fish Department employees spread rapidly across the state that afternoon of October 16, 1991. The plane, chartered by the department to track radio-collared grizzly bears, had left the Jackson Hole Airport at 8:30 a.m. and was due back by 11:40 a.m.

Gale-force winds had begun blowing across the mountains of northwestern Wyoming at mid-morning, and it was at first hoped that the aircraft had made a safe forced landing somewhere in the region. By sundown, however, there was still no word from the crew.

Aboard the lost aircraft were 28-year-old game warden Kirk Inberg, the department's grizzly bear conflict resolution specialist, 26-year-old bear biologist Kevin Roy, and experienced pilot Ray Austin, 47.

The missing plane was a white, blue and orange Maule M5-235 with identification number N19AR on its tail, owned by Western Air Research of Driggs, Idaho. It was fitted with the latest navigational and wildlife tracking equipment.

Austin was certified as a commercial pilot and rated for land, sea, helicopter and instrument flight. His flying record was substantial: 6,262 flight hours with 1,769 hours in the Maule itself. Ray had worked as a wildlife research pilot for the company for about a year and a half and had piloted hundreds of missions including wildlife radio-tracking and census flights and aerial support during forest fires.

Shortly after the Casper office of the Federal Aviation Agency reported there had been no word from the pilot to cancel or change his flight plan, Western Air Research had two planes and a helicopter in the air and heading towards the area.

Since it was thought the main purpose of the radio-tracking flight was to check on a wounded grizzly bear in the Mount Leidy and Spread Creek areas, the initial effort was in that vicinity.

That evening, a commercial airliner had reported receiving Emergency Locator Transmitter (ELT) signals while flying over the Gravel Peak vicinity.

An air and ground search of that area proved fruitless and it was thought the ELT reading had been from a false signal.

What followed was the most extensive search in Wyoming history. The hunt, led by the Teton County sheriff's office, would utilize 30 airplanes, seven helicopters, 150 volunteer ground searchers and numerous search and rescue teams.

As word of the missing aircraft reached the backcountry hunting camps, a number of sightings during the high winds of October 16 were reported by guides and hunters. That morning, several elk hunters in the remote Thorofare country had seen a low-flying light plane fitting the description being tossed around by strong winds. At the time, fierce ground zephyrs were blowing trees down all about the hunters. One hunter near Bridger Lake told of watching the plane flying low over Yellowstone Point on a course towards Jackson just after noon.

The lost plane was well equipped for an emergency. On board were two programmable, hand-held radios capable of receiving and transmitting emergency signals, a dash-mounted aircraft radio, an ELT and a manually-activated radio collar like the ones placed on grizzly bears. In addition to these electronic devices, the plane was equipped with flares, smoke grenades, sleeping bags, food enough to last for several days and first aid equipment. In spite of all the emergency and survival equipment on board, no confirmed signals were received.

All three members were experienced in wilderness survival. Also, Kirk and Kevin were familiar with the country they had likely crashed in. The lack of any sign led searchers and family members to conclude that the worst possible scenario had occurred and the crash had not been survivable.

Still, the search was expanded from predictable sites where the plane may have been to the entire 2,000-square-mile grizzly bear study area and beyond. Much of this rugged Greater Yellowstone region is remote, with extensive expanses of timbered mountains. Because of the backcountry sightings of the lost aircraft around its planned 11:40 a.m. return to the airport, it was thought possible the crew might have decided to extend the telemetry flight searching for radio-collared bears. However, a more likely scenario was that the aircraft, out of necessity, had attempted to leave the area of severe turbulence.

Certainly the news of the tragedy was a blow to all who knew the lost men. Each of them was dedicated to the wildlife cause. I knew Kirk quite well and had worked several grizzly-human conflicts with him. Just three weeks before the tragedy, while on wilderness patrol, I had bumped into his camp on Siggins Fork of Open Creek where he and two companions were trapping and radio-collaring grizzlies. While Kirk and I may have disagreed somewhat on certain bear research techniques, I never once doubted the man's sincerity and ability as a bear researcher. He knew and loved the grizzly and was 110 percent for the animal's recovery. Kirk talked and thought "grizzly" every waking moment. And anyone who didn't share his love for the great beast had best step aside.

Now, he was likely down there somewhere among his beloved bears.

The search continued for two weeks until prolonged severe winter weather and deepening snow cover finally shut down the massive operation for the winter. No trace of the plane or its crew had been found.

"He was really good at his job and he was doing what he wanted to do,

Kirk Inberg.
Photo: Wyoming Game and Fish Department

in some of the most beautiful parts of the country, a part of the country that he loved," said Judy Inberg, Kirk's mother. "He's always fought for grizzly bears. He was really dedicated to his job."

On October 10, 1992, nearly a year after the plane was lost, the game and fish department renamed its East Fork game winter range near Dubois "The Kirk Inberg-Kevin Roy Wildlife Habitat Management Area" to honor their memory and their commitment to duty.

A number of other searches for the lost aircraft and its crew were conducted after the initial 1991 effort, including a large-scale search in 1993.

Each season, after the snows had again melted from the wilderness mountains, hunters and anglers were reminded of the lost aircraft, and asked to keep an eye out for it during their travels.

In July of 1994, a concentrated ground search of the Yellowstone Point area just off the southeast corner of Yellowstone Park turned up no trace of the plane. The area was "the only place that really had any high probability at all that we never did finish," due to bad weather and rugged terrain during the original search, according to Teton County sheriff Roger Millward.

"This finally closes out everything we could possibly do in this search," he added. "I think the families feel the same way. We've made as much effort as we can possibly make until we get new clues." Those clues would come the next year.

An elk's final bugle led a Thermopolis hunter to the wreckage of the missing aircraft after a four-year search.

"We were actually just taking a walk," said Michelle Perry, who, along with friend Chris Greene of Worland, found the wreckage about a half mile from their camp on September 23, 1995, near the Soda Fork of the Buffalo River.

"What was really strange is that when Chris and I were walking, we came up on a knob hill and we heard a strange noise," Perry remembered. "It sounded kind of like a little whirlwind. We couldn't identify the noise, so we climbed the knob. We couldn't see anything, and it had started to snow. Then, we heard the bugle. I tried to get an answer. The elk didn't answer, so we walked east in the direction of the bugle. We walked right up to the plane.

"Then, I shot the elk, my baby five-point," Perry said. "You can walk within 60 yards of the aircraft and not know it's there."

The densely wooded terrain at the crash site above Soda Fork in the Teton Wilderness made the missing plane difficult to spot from the air. Photo: Fred Herbel, Wyoming Game and Fish Department

Aircraft wreckage, burned and rusting, at the crash site. Photo: Fred Herbel, Wyoming Game and Fish Department.

Ironically, the day after Perry and Greene found the plane, Perry's husband, Dan, and his friend Terry Johnson were following flags left by the women to the wreckage. Just as they reached the downed plane, a bull elk bugled and Johnson downed it with a 60-yard shot.

"It was definitely an eventful hunting trip," Michelle Perry said.

The Teton County crash site was 1,200 feet up very steep, heavily timbered terrain from the Soda Fork pack trail, four miles west of Crater Lake and a mile from the Fremont County line.

Investigators said it appeared the crash had happened quickly and possibly without time for the pilot to radio a problem. From the condition of plane's remains and the burned vegetation around it, it seemed the ensuing fire had melted and burned much of the surroundings.

Photos of the crash site showed the rusted skeleton of the small aircraft not visible from the air. Fred Herbel, an enforcement specialist for the game and fish, described the wreckage as "rusted tubing and a pile of debris" that did "not look like a normal airplane."

It appeared the plane had descended at about a 35 degree angle, clipped three trees, struck the ground and burned. Human remains were found in and around the wreckage, and indications were that all three passengers were killed upon impact. A plate bore the exact model number and serial number of the missing aircraft.

Tragically, just one month after the crash site was found, another Western Air Research aircraft crashed after losing a wing over the pilot's home in northwest Teton County. Pilot Fred Reed, the owner of the company, was killed in the mishap.

Flying is a dangerous part of a wildlife field professional's job. Aircraft used in wildlife work are usually working at low altitudes over uneven topography, where any mistake, mechanical failure or weather disturbance can spell disaster.

Wyoming Game and Fish Department pilot Richard "Dick" Miller was killed when his aircraft crashed into 11,007-foot Breccia Peak, north of Togwotee Pass, during a 1962 fall snowstorm. He had just completed a game census flight in the Jackson area, and at the time of the mishap was enroute, alone, back to his Riverton station. Several Wyoming game wardens and biologists have been seriously injured in air crashes while on duty.

Within the inter-mountain region, a good number of wildlife people have lost their lives due to air crashes. Many more have been injured by them. A fortunate few have walked away unscathed from aircraft crash-sites. Most veteran wildlife biologists and game wardens can relate at least one harrowing airborne experience.

Wild Journey

Since the 1950s when Montana state game employees first began using aircraft in earnest to count, chase and capture wildlife, there have been five fatal accidents in that state, and many more close calls.

A series of recent aircraft accidents has spurred Washington state wildlife officials to question whether the low-level flights over dangerous terrain are worth the risk. On November 7, 1998, two federal biologists conducting a waterfowl survey died when their plane hit a power line and crashed into the Columbia River in south-central Washington. Three days later, a respected helicopter pilot died while on his way to pick up Colville tribal biologists.

In January, 1999, three people were injured when their helicopter crashed along a hillside outside the northern Idaho town of Tensed. The crew had been surveying the winter elk population for the Coeur d'Alene tribe. This accident has prompted the Idaho Department of Fish and Game to reevaluate its need for the information provided by such flights.

Even with the potential for disaster, game departments are bound to continue their use of aircraft for wildlife research and law enforcement because of the unique advantages the method offers.

This Wild Game

Garbage In, Garbage Out

A bitter controversy raged during the late 1980s over the management of the Wyoming Range mule deer herd. Early in 1989, biologists' deer herd population computer models indicated 60,000 head of the animals then existed within that management area. This number was up 40,000 head from population models they had run on that herd just four years earlier. If this information was true, it meant that the department was way above its agreed-upon population objective for that area of 35,000 deer. The biologists declared that drastic measures must be taken to reduce the size of the herd.

Area game wardens, also charged with game management responsibilities, disagreed with the over-population notion because their field observations didn't reflect such a problem, and they claimed inaccurate data had been used in the computer models. Furthermore, they said, the severe 1988 drought had not favored the herd. The lack of forage that winter had caused considerable mortality throughout the deer herd.

This information failed to dissuade the scientists and they began publicly advocating, without full department support, for a major reduction in the herd by recommending multiple-bag-limit hunting seasons within the management unit.

This sparked a vicious and long-lasting dispute between the department and area sportsmen, who objected vehemently to the season proposals. Several retired game wardens and a retired department wildlife biologist, all familiar with the situation, joined the sportsmen in their opposition, declaring the deer herds could not withstand such liberal hunting seasons.

When legally required public meetings were held by game department personnel during the hunting season-setting process, the hearings became shouting matches. Most of those in attendance made strong objections to the multiple-bag limit deer seasons being proposed by the biologists.

Game wardens opposing the seasons were told to back off.

The wildlife scientists convinced game department and commission officials that the situation was critical, which caused them to approve, in the face of great opposition, the first of several multiple-bag limit hunting seasons.

In the Wyoming Range during each of the next two hunting seasons, a hunter could legally kill three deer, of which at least two had to be antlerless.

Sportsmen throughout the state continued to call for an end to the deer slaughter and they were outraged by the audacity displayed by the department. The Star Valley Wildlife Club cast a unanimous vote against the seasons.

In the middle of all this controversy, one game warden polled the landowners in his district and found 92 percent of them believed the deer herds couldn't support such liberal hunting seasons. He was soon told that this was not scientific information. Still, when landowners say there aren't too many deer, you can usually hang your hat on it!

Absolutely undaunted by this information, the biologists pushed for yet more liberal hunting seasons. Convincing the department that insufficient harvests had resulted from the three-deer bag limit seasons, the wildlife scientists, in 1991, set the most liberal deer hunting seasons ever held in the state of Wyoming.

That fall, a hunter was allowed to take a bag limit of ten mule deer in some parts of the Wyoming Range.

Statements made at public meetings before the season proved rather mild compared to acrid comments at hearings held after the close of the ridiculous hunting seasons. Many hunters testified they had felt extremely fortunate to harvest just one deer. Some hunters had failed to bag a deer in the area. Consensus at one post-season public meeting was that if the huge deer population necessary to justify a ten-deer bag limit actually existed, then even a road-hunter ought to be able to find a single deer.

Citizens placed phone calls to the governor's office and wrote a multitude of letters to the editors of several Wyoming newspapers demanding the resignations or removal of those responsible, especially the head biologist, for making the asinine management decision. Neither occurred. Some hunters called for future hunting season closures in the area since they claimed a huntable deer herd no longer existed there.

The game managers responsible for the bungled management professed no wrongdoing and implied publicly that hunters couldn't find deer because they were lazy and inept, and made other disparaging comments about them. As should have been expected, these comments made about the public by public servants infuriated everyone and served only to augment the dissension.

Curiously, a department release concerning the "Mule Deer Controversy" explained how 50 percent of the juvenile deer were lost in some Wyoming Range areas during the winter of 1992-3, and that a later spring storm had a devastating effect on yearlings and newborns.

As time passed, a few of those responsible for the mismanagement quietly hinted that faulty data may have been used in their deer herd population models.

This unfortunate game management debacle lost for the department much of the public confidence and backing that it had for years enjoyed. Yet it is a valuable lesson. Wildlife managers need to guard against becoming so full of themselves that they display absolute knowledge of the relatively new science of wildlife management.

Certainly the computer age is here to stay. And the technology is a blessing when properly used as a tool. The trouble is, many "game experts" now spend more time playing with computers than they do expanding their professional knowledge. In many ways a computer is like a dairy cow. Someone must constantly feed and milk it to keep things going in an orderly fashion. One must faithfully "feed" in new data, and "milk" out the old to keep everything up to snuff. This is all very time consuming.

Today's wildlife managers are "book-smart" and great technophiles. While this modern-age knowledge is now essential, it is merely the first step towards a productive wildlife management career. Good managers spend a great deal of time in the field, keeping up with the natural world and numerous relevant practical matters. Wildlife loses when game managers fail to acquire this additional education. The trouble is, this invaluable knowledge can't be gained while staring into a computer screen.

Nowadays, there are too many game managers who spend most of their work-year sitting in front of computers that do their thinking for them. Since these fellows seldom venture far afield, they must depend for their computer fodder on data sometimes collected by inexperienced biologist aides, and on biased hunter-harvest questionnaires. And game population field information from other sources may be discarded if it happens to indicate something other than desired by the head game management whiz.

Game managers are getting themselves locked into inaccurate game herd population computer models from one year to the next. Such faulty computer models have caused some embarrassing moments for game departments.

The use of flawed or "salted" data to manage wildlife is never acceptable. Information garnered from a computer is only as good as the data fed into it. It becomes too easy for some folks to manufacture information to make a computer model run. As they say, "Figures don't lie, but liars figure."

We are just beginning to learn something about wildlife. Until game managers know, precisely, all the intricate details of wildlife population dynamics, they should not pretend that game management is even close to being an exact science.

Society may need to be reminded that it was concerned sportsmen, landowners and old-time game wardens who brought the game herds back from the brink nearly a century ago, long before the emergence of the wildlife scientist. The country was replenished with big game animals, and up through the 1950's, game wardens used basic, yet reliable, game management strategies such as:

When foot hunters bitch, there are probably too few deer.

When road hunters don't bitch, there are probably
too many deer.

Landowners will tell you when there are either too
many or too few deer.

A desirable deer population has most likely been reached
when there is little grumbling from landowners and sportsmen.

These comments from the public, or lack of them, when tempered with a district warden's intimate knowledge of herd and habitat conditions, were criteria sufficient to set a satisfactory hunting season. A commonsense approach to game management was used successfully for many years.

Of course, the old so-called "seat of the pants" game management methodology, used alone, is too simple for today's confused world. Modern man must now complicate everything beyond his knowledge.

Future wildlife managers should give proper consideration to time-tested methods of game management. They must also strive to perfect methods for obtaining accurate game population data without harming that resource. And it should always be kept in mind that employees who display rude or arrogant demeanors serve only to disrupt the game management process.

There exists a long-standing rift between many North American wildlife biologists and game wardens. Some authorities would no doubt deny this, but they should know better. The underlying cause for this disaffection is the idea that most biologists are too liberal in their game management philosophies while most game wardens are accused of being too conservative in their management beliefs. The results are frequent clashes at in-house (and a few public) hunting season-setting meetings.

To be protective comes with a warden's calling. Seasoned game wardens, many of which have the same academic credentials as do biologists, tend to rely more on the obvious and common sense rather than questionable scientific rhetoric and formulas in their decision making. A wildlife law officer's conservative stance is most assuredly influenced by his year-round contact with wildlife, landowners, sportsmen, and outlaws, and other pertinent field experiences, engendering more "real-world" conditioning. Wardens often become hardened conservationists while following a poacher's bloody trail. A game warden would rather make a questionable game management call on the side of wildlife.

A fair blend of the two wildlife management philosophies works reasonably well.

Fishermen of the Cloth
or "Do As I Say, Not As I Do."

One evening I was patrolling the Little Big Horn River in northern Sheridan County. At a bend in the river, someone jumped up from the stream bank as if they had just been bitten by a snake! By that time in my career I was familiar with the maneuver: It was the age-old human reaction to getting caught doing something wrong. The man had seen me coming his way and had immediately scurried off a short distance to join a woman preparing a picnic meal. A child and a puppy were playing nearby.

The man fit the exact profile of someone caught fishing without a license so I approached the picnic area and asked the usual, "How's fishing?" "Oh," exclaimed the man, "we're not fishing, we're just enjoying nature this evening, and are about to partake in a picnic supper. Won't you please join us?" We exchanged the usual introductions and I learned that he was the pastor of the Southern Baptist Church in nearby Wyola, Montana. He expressed surprise to find out that I was a game warden. I thanked him for the offer to join them for hamburgers, but said that I had already eaten supper.

Leaving the preacher with his family, I walked directly to the spot on the river where he had made the swift movement. Along the bank lay an ancient split-bamboo fly-fishing pole and reel with line left in the water. As I reeled in the line, along with a small rainbow trout, I heard a voice behind me say, "Well, it looks like I'm caught!"

The preacher said that he had just wanted to try out the old fishing outfit. He said the pole had great sentimental value as it was handed down to him by his grandfather. He went on to apologize for fishing without a license and then fibbing about it. The parson told me that the Devil had made him do it!

The minister paid his fine, got his pole back, and went on to poach ... I mean, preaching, if not practicing, the Ten Commandments!

Another encounter with a fisherman of the cloth was on the Tongue River west of Dayton. One summer afternoon, I saw two fishermen wading in mid-stream. Upon reaching the river bank I could see that one of the anglers was a middle-aged man and the other a young lady. Both anglers were bedecked in the latest fly-fishing regalia and looked as if they had just stepped out of an Orvis catalog. When I asked to see their licenses, the distinguished-looking gentleman informed me that none was required because he was a rector of the Church of England in Canada, and that the young lady was his daughter. Since they were fishing on the Adamson Ranch, I asked him if rectors need not gain permission to enter upon private property also. In an indignant voice he exclaimed that he could fish without permission anywhere in Canada, and he presumed the same courtesy was extended to those of his faith down here. I told the guy that his faith was not among those religions that were exempt from license requirements under the Pious Fishermen Pact.

Of course no such pact existed but I played along with him, wondering just how far this "holier than thou" individual would go. He acted quite surprised when I said that each of them must post a $100 bond for the violation of fishing without licenses. The clergyman was a very good actor, and when he could see that the one line wasn't working, he switched to the old "no money" ploy. He said that since they were broke that they would just lay it out in jail. I told him the idea sounded good to me and to climb aboard for the ride to the courthouse. His daughter could follow us in their new car. Once there they could then either post a bond or spend time in the hoosegow, it mattered not to me!

The conniving old con artist tried yet one more ruse when he suggested that his comely 18-year-old daughter ride with me and that he would follow in the new car. No way, Jose! It was obvious there was no limit how far this guy would go to get out of a tight spot.

As the rector and I were heading to town with the daughter following in the new car, he said several times, "In the eyes of the Lord, I am not guilty!"

They found money in a sock for the bond.

Still another "religious experience" happened as I was patrolling on horse-back around Bridger Lake. Seeing a fisherman on the south side, I rode over that way. Dragging a stringer of fish behind him, the angler beat a hasty retreat into the nearby pines when he figured out who I might be.

Now it doesn't take a lawman's sixth sense to know something was not right. Since my horse was just a little faster than he was, I soon caught up with him in the timber. Dismounting, I could see the fishermen's stringer didn't hold over the legal limit of cutthroat trout for those waters, so I suspected that he did not have a fishing license.

When I asked to see his fishing license, he said with a slight Irish brogue, "I left it in my car at the Turpin Meadows trailhead." That location was 25 miles away on foot (he had hiked in) or horseback from Bridger Lake. I then asked him for some identification. He said that he had left all his credentials in his wallet at the trailhead. As I continued to ask questions, the angler finally found a gasoline credit card slip in his pocket and handed it to me. On the slip was the name Father John _____, Salt Lake City, Utah. I asked him if he was, in fact, a Catholic priest. He assured me that he was one indeed.

The man of the cloth hesitated when I asked him for the location of the agency where he purchased his Wyoming fishing license. Because priests don't lie, I knew there had to be another explanation for his hesitation, such as maybe an Alzheimer's problem. Really, though, I had learned quite a little

Bridger Lake in the Teton Wilderness. Photo: Dave Bragonier

about human nature by that time and was pretty sure I knew what his real problem was.

Like a parent talking to a child, I told the guy that there was a big difference between forgetting to bring your license with you and not having a license at all and then lying about it. So we began the questioning again. I asked him, "Do you have a fishing license?"

Looking at the ground, he replied, "No, I do not!"

I couldn't resist the temptation when I asked, "Don't you know that it's naughty to tell a lie?" He exclaimed, "I know, I know, I've been asking forgiveness!"

For those folks who may feel discriminated against, do not despair! All religions are well represented by their sporting clergy.

Is there an extra-warm clime somewhere for these guys?

How Many True Sportsmen?

There are millions of hunters and fishermen out there. But how many of them are true sportsmen? Webster defines a sportsman as, "One who exhibits qualities especially esteemed in those who engage in sports, as fairness, courtesy, good temper, etc."

How many hunters and fishermen do you know (yes, including yourself) who practice strict ethical standards while pursuing their sport? Before answering that question you may wish to read on.

It's just before dark on the last day of the deer season as you travel empty-handed down a back road towards home. You spot a decent buck a few yards off the road on posted private land, but there's not enough shooting-light left to obtain permission from the landowner who doesn't live nearby. No other vehicles or hunters are in the area and the chances of getting caught seem remote. Would you shoot the deer?

If you honestly wouldn't shoot the deer – congratulations – you rank among a handful of the hunting fraternity! However, if you are a common or what I like to call generic hunter, given the circumstances, you would most likely shoot the buck from the vehicle and/or road, and then hastily remove the carcass from the private property and dress it elsewhere. A minimum of two Wyoming game laws would probably have been violated during this illegal activity: Shooting from vehicle/road, and trespassing to hunt.

Those who doubt that there are so few true sportsmen need only visit with a game warden who has helped with wildlife decoy sting operations to become believers.

The nation's game wardens are presently using simulated wildlife decoys to address a number of chronic law enforcement problems such as hunters shooting from public roads, hunting in closed areas, taking wildlife out of season and using artificial light to take wildlife. These decoys may simulate whatever wildlife species hunters take illegal advantage of.

Most states presently have laws addressing the use of simulated wildlife decoys in law enforcement. In 1995, the Wyoming legislature passed legislation making it illegal to attempt to take simulated wildlife in violation of any law or regulation concerning the hunting or taking of the wildlife being simulated. Conviction of violating this law carries the same penalty as is prescribed for the unlawful taking of the wildlife being simulated.

Some hunters cry foul and say wildlife decoy sting operations are entrapping innocent sportsmen. However, the courts have ruled that as long as no one is encouraged to shoot decoys, the mere presence of an opportunity to take a wild animal does not constitute entrapment.

An elk decoy kept several game wardens hopping during a recent opening day of elk season in Wyoming's Medicine Bow National Forest. In just six hours the officers wrote 21 citations and several warning tickets to persons shooting the decoy from a public road and/or vehicle.

Shortly thereafter, game department law enforcement officers used a deer decoy during the Baggs deer season. There were 11 violations, ranging from shooting from a public road to hunting after hours and using artificial light.

Russ Pollard, law enforcement coordinator for the Wyoming Game and Fish Department, sums up decoy sting operations quite well when he states, "It puts the violator, Game and Fish and the decoy in the same place at the same time, you don't spend lots of time and nothing is killed. That's the beauty of it!"

The use of wildlife decoys by game law enforcement agencies is another method of apprehending those who intentionally violate game laws. Such operations educate people and save wildlife.

So why do hunters cast aside what they were taught in hunter-safety class and intentionally violate game laws? Must man hunt because of a primitive desire to draw blood as some folks would suggest? Let's hope anti-hunters are wrong when they say hunters must kill to express their masculinity!

One thing is for sure: it is impossible to determine in a classroom environment what a hunter is liable to do in the hunting field.

Some years back I investigated a hunting casualty in the Big Horn Mountains. A deer hunter had somehow mistaken another hunter, who was dressed from head to foot in hunter-red clothing, for a deer. The accident had occurred at a distance of about 100 yards during legal shooting hours but before sunrise on an overcast day. Nothing had obstructed the shooter's sight-picture, but the victim had been standing next to some chokecherry bushes at the time of the shooting. Both the shooter and his wife – who was also hunting and standing next to him when he fired the shot – swore they thought the victim was a mule deer buck! The shooter, a banker by profession, probably had good judgment in other matters. Some folks can see – in their mind's-eye – anything they wish to see!

Wild Journey

For obvious reasons, the word "sportsman" will be used sparingly on the following pages.

Hunters now depend, almost entirely, upon modern conveyances while in pursuit of the quarry and never stray far afoot. These latter-day sportsmen ravage the countryside with their four-wheel-drives and work harder – digging, pushing, pulling, cutting and winching to get their vehicles into pristine locations – than if they had walked or ridden horses in! The ugly two-track scars cause erosion and soon become permanent landmarks. And it's always the other guy who did it. Unwise land-use by hunters seems to indicate a total lack of appreciation for natural beauty and suggests that bagging game means everything to them. If ever hunting is banned, this kind of mentality will deserve much of the credit!

Hunting-sports writers should be placing more emphasis on the urgent need to upgrade hunters rather than discussing which of the latest elephant guns and land-yachts will best reduce a critter to meat. They keep repeating the same old stories about shooting great distances at game animals without properly explaining the high risk of cripple-loss involved with such a practice. The generic hunter spends little time searching for a wounded animal. The ancient art of tracking, an essential element in proper hunting skills, is unknown to most of today's nimrods.

Fishing editors are touting any and all gadgetry capable of assisting with high-tech warfare on fish. Sonar-GPS combos now enable fishers in one operation to locate and mark – exactly – the quarry's favorite hangouts. Beginning anglers hear precious little about fishing's sacred moments. Sportfishing's future would best be served if youngsters heard more about the virtues of simple, low-impact fishing for enjoyment and less high-tonnage babble from professional sportfishers with their tournament-mentality chatter.

And fishermen don't even know their fish! A recent Idaho Department of Fish and Game study done in the Boise River drainage which contains the protected bull trout, among other trout species, proved the point. Biologists polled fishers on those streams and determined that as many as 70 percent of all anglers couldn't tell the bull trout from other trout species. Many of them didn't know the physical differences among trout and grayling, squawfish or whitefish! The study showed that fly-fishing aficionados were most likely to correctly identify bull trout, but even then, barely half did. Not even a third of those using artificial lures and less than a fifth of the bait fishermen identified the threatened fish.

The Idaho study's basic findings can almost certainly be applied to fishermen elsewhere, and when the majority of sportfishers are unable to identify fish they catch, it presents a serious threat to both their sport and native fisheries.

Nearly 40 years of game wardening has totally convinced me that barely 10 percent of all hunters and fishers fit the true sportsman category! A firm 85 percent of all would-be sportsmen are mere generic hunters/fishers. The remaining 5 percent are professional poachers, the low-lifes who poach wildlife year-round and are likely to make part or all of their living doing so. This is not to say that attitudes regarding poaching haven't changed for the better during this time. They have. But, obviously, major improvement is still needed. The actions of the hunting and fishing majority are giving anti-hunters the ammunition they want in their attempt to trash the sports.

A true sportsman practices a very high ethical standard, abides by all laws and can enjoy an outdoor experience without firing a shot. He can usually be found hunting on foot or horseback away from the crowds, roads and vehicles. He is adept at the primitive craft of hunting, and game is seldom lost once he shoots.

Why is it that a diversity of folks, who wouldn't otherwise consciously violate the law, intentionally and willfully break game regulations?

A judge from Houston, Texas, and his 11-year-old son (14 was the legal age to hunt big game) both swore false oaths to obtain resident Wyoming deer licenses after arriving in the state. While attempting to explain why he did it to Park County justice of the peace Richard Day, the Texas magistrate said, "When I found they were sold out of non-resident licenses I became so angry that I made the false statement and told my son to do the same so that we could go hunting!" When interviewed by a reporter back in Houston, the convicted judge said, "I didn't swear falsely – I wouldn't do that – I thought it would be just like a $100 fine for shooting a duck too early!"

The same Wyoming judge heard a prosecuting attorney from Mount Dora, Florida, testify as follows, "I thought it would be O.K. to hunt on a dead man's license. He wasn't going to use it!" Of course the corrupt lawyer also used the deceased hunter's name while on the outfitted elk and deer hunt.

A Cody school's student counselor shot a deer during closed season. And remember the Kansas sheriff who jacklighted and abandoned a deer? More recently, a Wyoming game and fish department director lost his job after he was caught and convicted of fishing without a license. And the list goes on and on.

Most poaching occurs during hunting seasons. While the majority of hunters do not take game out of season, they think nothing of "in season" violations such as shooting someone else's deer or taking an occasional over limit of birds. Game taken illegally during the season is still poaching, pure and simple! And when these clowns go on a hunt with their children in tow, they are guaranteeing the perpetuation of illegal conduct in the field. The human race certainly is one of the few forms of life that will foul its own nest. Slob hunters are an imminent threat to the sport.

It will be non-hunters, not anti-hunters, who will likely decide the fate of hunting. There are many more non-hunters out there than all other groups put together, and their numbers are steadily growing while hunters are becoming fewer. Most of them are presently not opposed to hunting. However, continued unethical behavior among the hunting community could swing their vote against the sport.

On the other hand, it was the American sporthunter who first called for game laws and game departments to protect wildlife after market and subsistence hunting had ravaged it during the 19th century. Hunters and fishermen remain wildlife's strongest advocates, doling out millions of dollars each year through donations and license purchases for its habitat and management.

To date, what little the anti-hunting crowd has contributed towards genuine wildlife conservation is dwarfed when compared to that of the hunting and fishing fraternity. However, there is still much to be done by all true friends of animals. The country truly needs more defenders of wildlife habitat.

The degradation and loss of wildlife habitat will reduce game populations, which in turn will lower hunting opportunities. This, coupled with continued disrespect shown by hunters for game laws, is likely to spell disaster to the sport of hunting.

Still, compared to disease and famine, ethical hunting remains the gentlest form of wildlife population control.

What a dilemma!

Hunters and anglers have a bright future only if they begin displaying a great deal more respect for the land, wildlife and the law. In the past they have led the wildlife conservation effort. In the future they must strive much harder at saving their sport!

*TRUE SPORTSMAN (10%)

Makes a conscientious effort to know game regulations and hunt area.
Does not tolerate "party hunting" (You shoot mine – I'll shoot yours)
or other illegal practices.
Would rather pass up a shot than take a chance and make a mistake.
Does not need to "make a kill" in order to enjoy a day in the field.
Is not just interested in the "target" species, but also enjoys nature
in general.
Chooses hunting partners who also have high ethical standards.
Often stops short of a full limit of birds or fish.
Has a good knowledge of the quarry species and usually other
wildlife as well.
Handles firearms efficiently and safely.
Reports violations of the law in a timely manner.
Can occasionally be observed picking up someone else's litter.

**GENERIC HUNTER/FISHER (85%)

Usually has a poor knowledge of the game regulations and/or the hunt
area boundaries.
His number one priority is to "make a kill!"
Will often shoot from a vehicle/road or commit other violations to help
assure success.
Usually is a willing participant in the "party hunting" practice.
Occasionally takes advantage of a "good" day and bags an over limit.
Prone to litter the countryside.
Loves to boast about his hunting prowess, and enjoys displaying his kills.

***PROFESSIONAL POACHER (5%)

Has no hunting ethics and disregards game regulations and laws
in general.
Poaches both during and out of season.
Makes a practice of taking more than his share of wildlife.
Obeys only those rules and regulations essential for survival – such as
possessing a hunting license to display if necessary.
Usually has a good working knowledge of the target species only.
Displays little interest in wildlife having no value to him.
May be in the illicit wildlife market.
Likely to be a dangerous adversary to law enforcement officers.
Is not prone to enjoy a sunset.

* Percentage may be too high. Please allow for error.
** Having one or more of this category's traits places a hunter here.
*** Percentage may be too low. Please allow for error.

Bibliography

In the writing of *Wild Journey*, the author's personal journals and records were frequently consulted.

Bill Daniels, Mountain Man
Wyoming Wildlife Magazine, Wyoming Game and Fish Department:
7/39, 12/39, 5/47, 6/47, 7/47, 10/47, 12/47, 4/48

The Beginning of a Career
Anderson, Chester C. 1958. The Elk of Jackson Hole. Bulletin No. 10.
    Wyoming Game and Fish Commission, Cheyenne
Blair, Neal. 1987. *The History of Wildlife Management in Wyoming.*
    Wyoming Game and Fish Department. Cheyenne

Sedgwick County's Finest
Wyoming Game and Fish Department arrest records

Punchin' Elk
Wyoming Wildlife, Wyoming Game and Fish Department, April, 1969
Blair, Neal, 1987, *The History of Wildlife Management in Wyoming.*
    Wyoming Game and Fish Department. Cheyenne.
King, Calvin L. 1963. *Reestablishing Elk in the Bighorn Mountains of*
    Wyoming. Wyoming Game and Fish Department. Cheyenne.

You Owe Us!
Wyoming Game and Fish Department arrest records
United States Forest Service map of Bighorn Forest, 1957
Safari Magazine, Safari Club International, November/December, 1998
Trophy Hunter Magazine, Winter, 1998
Newspaper articles: The Billings (Montana) Gazette, The Casper
(Wyoming) Star-Tribune

A Stacked Deck
Wyoming Game and Fish Department arrest records

Bullheaded
Blair, Neal. 1987. *The History of Wildlife Management in Wyoming.*
    Wyoming Game and Fish Department. Cheyenne.
King, Calvin L. 1963. *Reestablishing Elk in the Bighorn Mountains of*

Wyoming. Wyoming Game and Fish Department. Cheyenne. Wyoming Wildlife Magazine. Wyoming Game and Fish Department. June 1969.
Newspaper article: The Sheridan (Wyoming) Press

The Long Season
Wyoming Game and Fish Department Arrest Records
Newspaper articles: The Billings (Montana) Gazette, The Casper (Wyoming) Star-Tribune, The Cody (Wyoming) Enterprise

The Black Marketeers
Wyoming Game and Fish Department Arrest Records
Standard appraisals and application for Safari Club International members hunt and trophy replacement insurance, 1992
Wyoming Wildlife News, Wyoming Game and Fish Department, May/June 1996, January/February, 1998 and March/April, 1998
Wyoming Wildlife Magazine, Wyoming Game and Fish Department, November, 1984
Newspaper articles: The Billings (Montana) Gazette, The Casper (Wyoming) Star-Tribune, The Cody (Wyoming) Enterprise

Those Damned Deer
Wildlife Damage Summary, Wyoming Game and Fish Department, 2/98
Wyoming Game and Fish Department Laws, 1997

The Moose Slayers
Wyoming Game and Fish Department Arrest Records
Seton, Ernest Thompson. *Lives of Game Animals.* Volume 111, Garden City and New York. Doubleday, Doran and Company, Inc. 1929
Newspaper Article: The Casper (Wyoming) Star-Tribune

A Day to Remember
Newspaper article: The Casper (Wyoming) Star-Tribune

"Burn, Baby, Burn!"
Summary of Public Comments on the Fire Management Policy Report, April 1989, U.S. Department of Agriculture and U.S. Department of Interior
Final Report on Fire Management Policy, May 5, 1989, U.S. Department of Agriculture and U.S. Department of Interior

Newspaper articles: The Billings (Montana) Gazette, The Casper
    (Wyoming) Star-Tribune, The Cody (Wyoming) Enterprise

The Riddle of Yellowstone's Lake Trout
Simon, J.R. *Yellowstone Fishes*. Yellowstone Library and Museum
    Association, Yellowstone National Park, Wyoming. 1939
Simon, J.R. *Wyoming Fishes*. Wyoming Game and Fish Department. 1951
Newspaper articles: The Billings (Montana) Gazette

What Have We Done to the Grizzly Bear?
On the Trail in Grizzly Country
Craighead, Frank C, Jr., *Track of the Grizzly*. San Francisco, Sierra Club
    Books. 1979
Herrero, Stephen. *Bear Attacks, Their Causes and Avoidance*. Winchester
    Press. Piscataway, NJ. 1985
Mills, Enos A. *The Grizzly: Our Greatest Wild Animal*. Boston and New
    York. Houghton Mifflin Company. 1919.
Russell, Andy. *Grizzly Country*. New York. Alfred A. Knopf. 1968.
Seton, Ernest Thompson. *Lives of Game Animals*. Volume II - Part I.
    Garden City and New York. Doubleday, Doran and Company,
    Inc. 1929.
Wright, William Henry. *The Grizzly Bear*. New York. Charles Scribner's. 1909.
Bear management in Glacier National Park, A Summary of, 1960-1994.
    National Park Service. 11/96
Grizzly Bear Mortalities in the Yellowstone Ecosystem 1959-1987.
    Montana Department of Fish, Wildlife and Parks.
Grizzly Bear Attacks At Granite Park and Trout Lake in Glacier Nat'l Park.
    National Park Service. US Department of the Interior. August 13,
    1967.
Numerous Interagency Grizzly Bear Study Team Reports
National Fish and Wildlife Foundation Report 11/88
Wyoming Game and Fish Department Arrest Records.
Newspaper Articles:
"Cody man fined $800 for killing grizzly." Cody Enterprise. September 14, 1977.
"Hunt guide fined for killing grizzly."Billings Gazette. October 2, 1980.
"The Bear Facts." Bozeman Daily Chronicle. October 3, 1982.
"Man fined $5000 for killing a grizzly." Billings Gazette. February 5, 1983.
"Yellowstone bear kills camper." Billings Gazette. August 2, 1984.
"Bear killing and mauling mar Park's record." Cody Enterprise. August 6,
    1984.

"Outdoorsman blames drugs for bears' fury." Billings Gazette. August 15, 1984.

"Drugs aren't driving grizzlies crazy." Billings Gazette. September 23, 1984.

"Mauling victim: 'He was at me in two bounds'." Jackson Hole News. October 3,1984.

"Three hunters sentenced for killing grizzly." Casper Star-Tribune. January 26, 1989.

"Grizzly bear mauls Cody man." Casper Star-Tribune. September 14, 1990.

"Bear attacks rising for several reasons." Billings Gazette. October 12, 1992.

"Mauled hunter wounds griz." Cody Enterprise. September 9, 1992

"Elk hunters kill charging grizzly." Billings Gazette. October 12, 1993.

"Yellowstone bear mauls Gillette man." Casper Star-Tribune. July 19, 1994

"This bear wanted to kill me." Billings Gazette. July 21, 1994.

"Bear inflicted more terror than pain." Billings Gazette. August 30, 1994

"Humans and bears have a record year of run-ins." Casper Star-Tribune. November 6, 1994

"Casper man survives mauling by grizzly." Billings Gazette. September 21, 1994

"Bear Aggression weather linked." Billings Gazette. July 6, 1995.

"Native Alaskans: 'Bear research methods offensive'." Casper Star-Tribune. July 22, 1995.

"Anger gave hunter strength to live." Billings Gazette. September 25, 1995.

"Hunters kill grizzly near Dubois." Casper Star-Tribune. September 26, 1996.

"U.S. officials probe 2 killings of grizzies." Billings Gazette. September 29, 1996.

"New grizzly data suggests 'baby boom'." Casper Star-Tribune. October 3, 1996.

"Nuisance grizzly killed." Casper Star-Tribune. October 11, 1996.

"Hunting guide kills grizzly that mauled woman." Billings Gazette. November 9, 1996.

"Guide describes grizzly bear attack." Billings Gazette. November 12, 1996.

"Yellowstone grizzly bears produce record cub numbers." Powell Tribune. December 3, 1996.

"Lawsuit cuts into grizzly recovery, says official." Casper Star-Tribune. January 23, 1997.

"Grizzly bears feed on plane crash victims." Billings Gazette.
	June 19, 1998.
"Grizzlies kill Glacier Park hiker and scavenge his remains."
	Billings Gazette. June 19, 1998.
"Wanted bear threatens hikers; rangers resume hunt." Billings Gazette.
	June 26, 1998.
"Troublesome grizzly bear shot at Glacier National Park."
	Casper Star-Tribune. June 27, 1998.

Murders in the Sierra Madre
Carbon County Historical Society Meeting Notes, Rawlins, WY, 8/12/95
Biennial Report of William T. Judkins, Wyoming State Game Warden,
	1919-1920
U. S. Weather Bureau Record for October - November, 1945.
Wyoming Game and Fish Department Arrest Records.
Wyoming Wildlife Magazine, Wyoming Game and Fish Department,
	January, 1946.
Newspaper articles: The Denver (Colorado) Post, The Rawlins (Wyoming)
	Republican-Bulletin, The Thermopolis (Wyoming) Record

Overdue
The Gaffer (Wyoming Game and Fish Department employee publication)
	January 1993
Wyoming Wildlife News, Wyoming Game and Fish Department, January-
	February 1992, November-December 1995
Newspaper Articles: The Billings (Montana) Gazette, The Casper
	(Wyoming) Star-Tribune

Garbage In, Garbage Out
Newspaper articles: The Casper (Wyoming) Star-Tribune

How Many True Sportsmen?
Wyoming Game and Fish Department arrest records.
International Game Warden Magazine, Winter, 1997-1998
Wyoming Wildlife News, Wyoming Game and Fish Department,
	May/June, 1996, January/February 1998 and March/April 1998
Newspaper articles: The Billings (Montana) Gazette, The Cody
	(Wyoming) Enterprise, The Casper (Wyoming) Star-Tribune

Author with Moonshine at the game and fish Thorofare patrol cabin. Photo: Terry Cleveland

About the Author

A Wyoming Law Enforcement Academy graduate, Dave Bragonier studied forestry for a time and later earned a police science degree. He began his 35-year game warden career in Jackson Hole, Wyoming and, after assignments elsewhere in the state, held the Cody warden position for 21 years.

Dave was chosen Wyoming's 1973 Wildlife Officer of the Year by Shikar Safari Club International. In 1990, he received special recognition from the North American Wildlife Enforcement Officers Association. He is past president of both the Wyoming Game Wardens Association and the Wyoming Peace Officers Association.

Dave and his wife now live on their farm near Powell, Wyoming, where they keep busy and enjoy watching the wild inhabitants of a wetland habitat they developed there.

Marilyn Bragonier McCarthy ?
307-754-5686

Dave Bragonier 307-254-0269
Good Wolves
Bad Wolves